CORNWALL PUBLIC LIBRARY

D0672884

You'd Better Not Die or I'll Kill You

DISCARD

CORNWALL PUBLIC LIBRARY
395 HUDSON STREET
CORNWALL, NY 12518

FEB 1 8 2013

You'd Better Not Die or I'll Kill You

- - - - - - - - - - - - -

A Caregiver's Survival Guide to Keeping You
in Good Health and Good Spirits

JANE HELLER

CORNWALL PUBLIC LIBRARY
395 HUDSON STREET
CORNWALL, NY 12518

CHRONICLE BOOKS
SAN FRANCISCO

ALSO BY JANE HELLER:

FICTION
Clean Sweep (formerly Cha Cha Cha)
The Club
Infernal Affairs
Princess Charming
Crystal Clear
Sis Boom Bah
Name Dropping
Female Intelligence

The Secret Ingredient
Lucky Stars
Best Enemies
An Ex to Grind
Some Nerve

NONFICTION
Confessions of a She-Fan: The Course of True
Love with the New York Yankees

Copyright © 2012 by Jane Heller.
All rights reserved. No part of this book may be reproduced
in any form without written permission from the publisher.

Library of Congress Cataloging-in-Publication Data:
Heller, Jane.
  You'd better not die or I'll kill you : a caregiver's survival guide to keeping you in good health
and good spirits / Jane Heller.
    p. cm.
  ISBN 978-1-4521-0753-0
1. Heller, Jane--Humor. 2. Women caregivers--United States--Biography. 3. Caregivers--
Family relationships--Popular works. 4. Crohn's disease--Treatment--Popular works. I. Title.

RT61.H44 2012
362'.0425092--dc23
[B]

2012008156

Manufactured in China

Designed by *Jennifer Tolo Pierce*

10 9 8 7 6 5 4 3 2 1

Chronicle Books LLC
680 Second Street
San Francisco, California 94107
www.chroniclebooks.com

For Michael Forester,
my brave husband and best friend

- - - - - - - - - - - - - -

Table of Contents

Introduction 8

CHAPTER 1: What Is a Caregiver Anyway? 19

CHAPTER 2: Navigating Past the Freak-Out 32

CHAPTER 3: Making Emergency Room Visits
and Insanity Mutually Exclusive 49

CHAPTER 4: Doctors—Can't Live with 'Em,
Can't Live Without 'Em 60

CHAPTER 5: How to Turn Even the Crankiest Nurses/
Aides/Medical Personnel into Buddies 71

CHAPTER 6: When Loved Ones Take on a Different
Personality and You Start Wishing
They'd Disappear 80

CHAPTER 7: How to Wait Out Waiting Rooms 92

CHAPTER 8: The Hospital Room Etiquette
Miss Manners Never Told Us About 97

CHAPTER 9: Who's the Boss of Me? 101

CHAPTER 10: Getting on the Same Page as that Sister Who
Drives You Nuts (and Other Family Matters) 108

CHAPTER 11: Who Knew Friends Could Be So . . .
Unfriendly? 117

CHAPTER 12: Does Working Mean You Don't Care
or Does Caring Mean You Don't Work? 125

CHAPTER 13: The Home Health-Care Invasion 131

CHAPTER 14: Using the *F* Word, as in *Facility* 142

CHAPTER 15: Finding a Shoulder—or Ten—to Lean On.......... 155

CHAPTER 16: "Caregiver Sleep" Doesn't Have to
Be an Oxymoron 161

CHAPTER 17: The Great Escape—Taking a
Mental Vacation 166

CHAPTER 18: Being a Crybaby Isn't Necessarily
a Bad Thing 173

CHAPTER 19: Sometimes Laughter Isn't the Best Medicine—
It's the Only Medicine 177

CHAPTER 20: Just Breathe. Or Meditate. Or Both. 187

CHAPTER 21: Who Has Time to Cook a Healthy Meal?
We Do. 197

CHAPTER 22: The Exercise Conundrum 208

CHAPTER 23: Sex? Romance? Is Anybody Getting Any? 216

CHAPTER 24: When to See a Shrink 225

CHAPTER 25: "Spiritual Care" Isn't Necessarily Just
for the Spiritual 234

CHAPTER 26: Getting Through the Goodbye 241

CHAPTER 27: Yes, There Are Silver Linings 257

CHAPTER 28: When Caregiver Becomes Caregivee 269

CHAPTER 29: Famous Last Words 281

Acknowledgments 288

Introduction

"I can't take the pain!" Michael wailed. "Just get a gun and shoot me already!"

My then-boyfriend-now-husband scared the hell out of me that day in 1991, both because he wasn't the type to wail and because he was suggesting that I do something pretty Kevorkian-esque. In the eight months since he'd moved into my Connecticut house, I had never heard him raise his voice, much less beg for assisted suicide. Besides, I didn't own a firearm, not even one of those benign-looking mini-revolvers you can carry around in your handbag like a BlackBerry. The one and only time I fired a gun was during a college fraternity party at a "gentleman's farm" in Virginia. Everyone was taking part in something called skeet shooting, which, as a Jewess from Scarsdale, was as foreign to me as doing my own nails. My date showed me how to hold the rifle, I pulled the trigger, and I was blasted backward with such force that the hole in the ground is probably still there.

"Should I call an ambulance?" I said to Michael, not having a clue what I was supposed to do. I was a writer, not a doctor, and my nurturing skills were nonexistent. I didn't have kids. I didn't have pets. I didn't even have plants except for polyester ones, and even they looked wilted.

All I knew was what Michael had told me early in our courtship (in the most offhand, who-cares way) that he had something called Crohn's disease, which, I later learned, is an autoimmune disease of the gastrointestinal tract whose trademarks are—wait for it—abdominal pain, diarrhea, nausea, vomiting, rectal bleeding, intestinal blockage, osteoporosis, neuropathy, skin rashes, clubbing of the fingers, and severe depression. Since he had exhibited virtually none of the above atrocities and assured me that he'd been in remission for years, I paid little attention back then. We were in love, wildly attracted to each other, eager to be married and begin our sure-to-be-blissful future together.

Clearly, I was delusional.

"No ambulance!" yelled Michael. "Do you hear me?"

They could hear him in Azerbaijan.

He continued to thrash around on our living room sofa and I continued to circle him as if he were an explosive about to go off, and our housekeeper, an extremely focused Peruvian woman named Maria, continued to vacuum the carpet under our feet since it was her day to clean and I hadn't canceled, due to the sudden onset of Michael's condition.

"I'll take your temperature again," I said, feeling the need to do something, anything. I grabbed the thermometer and stuck it under his tongue. The verdict: his fever had spiked to 105.

"I'm so cold," he said, shaking now, convulsing.

Enough was enough. Even a dip like me knew it was time to call 911.

As Maria and I waited for the EMT guys, I tried to figure out what, exactly, had happened to my beloved. It was his head that was killing him, not his gut, and he said he felt as if someone had broken his legs. The fever could be causing the head and body aches, but what was causing the fever?

And then it hit me: the pills he'd been taking for the past month. He'd gone to a new gastroenterologist who'd put him on a drug called 6-MP. Could he be having a reaction to the medication?

I offered up my theory to the EMT guys when they arrived. They nodded and called me "ma'am" and looked like a cross between firemen and backup dancers for Lady Gaga, but they were more interested in swaddling Michael in blankets and lifting him onto a gurney than in listening to my chatter.

I backed away, gave them space, and wondered what I'd gotten myself into.

Growing up with a mother who had nursed two sick husbands (my father had brain cancer, my stepfather had complications from epilepsy), I had vowed to marry for health—to avoid being saddled with a mate who would require me to become that most dreaded of all things: a caregiver. What I'm saying is that the last— I mean, the very last—thing I was looking for in a man was a medical flaw. I would rather have married a crocodile.

Not that I didn't admire my mother's devotion as well as her lack of squeamishness when it came to seizures, bedpans, and vomit. (I had a thing about hurling—was terrified of doing it, being around someone doing it, even sitting through a movie in which someone was doing it.) I thought she was heroic, really I did, but I had no desire to follow in her footsteps. I had seen entirely too much dropping dead on the part of men and was looking for a guy who would hang around. When I met Michael, a tanned, lean, physically fit photographer who was so vigorous he had crewed on a 1920s schooner, sailed it to the Caribbean twice, and even survived a fall overboard into the Atlantic during a nor'easter, I said to myself, "*Woohoo.* Here's a live one."

So much for that, I thought now, as the gurney transporting Michael made its way down the stairs and out to our narrow street—at the very same moment that an extremely large van pulled up to the house.

"Heller residence?" the driver called out the window.

My heart lurched. I had completely forgotten about the boat—the do-it-yourself kit for a little woody dinghy that I'd ordered from *Wooden Boat* magazine as a surprise for Michael's birthday. He'd been eyeing it for weeks and I couldn't wait until it came. I just didn't expect it to come while he was being carted off to an emergency room.

I jumped into the street and started directing traffic and tried not to have a nervous breakdown. I convinced the driver to unload the boat and leave it in the garage under Maria's supervision, then climbed into the front seat of the ambulance, and sped away to the hospital.

Michael was in the back being "worked on," and I kept craning my neck to check on him. And then I started crying—loud, heavy, ridiculously wet sobs—and blubbered, "Please tell me he'll be all right."

"Don't worry," said the ambulance driver, becoming the first person to utter what would become a lifetime of "Don't worry's."

There was more fun to be had at the hospital. Since cell phones weren't as commonplace as they are now (plus they were the size of suitcases), I had to call Michael's gastro doc from a pay phone in the emergency room. I didn't reach him, naturally, because he was a Very Important Doctor, but his resident took my call.

"Could it be a reaction to the 6-MP?" I asked.

"Doubtful." He chuckled derisively, as if I'd just asked him if cigarettes were good for you. "It doesn't present that way."

"Well, it did *present* that way," I said.

"Let's see what happens when he's off the drug," he said.

What happened when Michael was off the drug was that I had been correct in my diagnosis: his fever vanished along with his body aches and it was, indeed, the 6-MP that had caused a reaction.

"Thanks for taking such good care of me," Michael said as he was being discharged.

"No big deal," I said, not in an attempt to be modest but because I wanted to block out the whole episode and go back to being a garden-variety woman in love.

Good try, Jane.

I had lost my caregiver virginity and there was no going back.

Crohn's, it turned out, was hardly "no big deal." Michael had been hospitalized nearly seventy-five times before I met him and was, in hospital parlance, "a frequent flier." He'd had intestinal obstructions and complications from surgeries and, as if Crohn's wasn't nasty enough, he got kidney stones a lot—like often enough to gravel a driveway. Oh, and did I mention that all he did was vomit? If there were a reality show called *American Hurler*, he'd win by a landslide.

I was tempted to bolt upon learning all these tidbits. I was tempted to tell *him* to bolt. I was tempted to say, "Sorry, dude, but I'm not cut out to be the wife of a man with all your medical issues." (Okay, I wouldn't have used the word *dude* back then. I wouldn't have used the word *issues* either; white men from Fairfield County weren't dudes and issues were known as problems.)

I should add here that I'd been married twice before, speaking of bolting.

My first husband was a charming guy with whom I'd gone to high school. We were young. We played a lot of tennis at the country club where both our families were members. We invited other similarly overprivileged couples to our Manhattan apartment for fondue. We were divorced within a year because we both realized that we had merely entered into a Starter Marriage and there was no point in pretending otherwise.

My second husband was a grownup—a divorced professional with two young children and a sweet disposition. We got together during the Greed-Is-Good '80s, built a 6,000-square-foot house in the suburbs, traveled to sprawling resorts of the type that offer villas with private "plunge pools," and dressed well. When the stock market went bust, so did our marriage.

And then I met Michael, who didn't have money but did have health (or so I thought). I predicted to anyone who'd listen, "Third time's the charm." What could possibly go wrong this time?

When I found out about his Crohn's—really let it sink in that we were talking about a chronic illness that would not only never go away but would probably get worse—I saw my life flash before me. (For some reason, these life-flashing-before-me fantasies were like clips from classic Bette Davis movies; I would gaze at Michael and deliver a line from, say, *Now, Voyager*: "Oh, Jerry. Don't let's ask for the moon. We have the stars.") I saw only tragedy and melodrama, with me as the long-suffering heroine.

But instead of bolting, I burrowed in. I suckered myself into thinking our romance was so special that our "happy vibes" would bolster his faulty immune system, that he would thrive once we were legally bound to each other, that love really would conquer all. And so, in the face of the evidence, I married him.

Over the next twenty years, Michael and I settled into a pattern. He'd suffer through his hospitalizations and/or surgeries (uncannily occurring over national holidays when doctors are playing golf in Palm Springs or skiing in Aspen or frolicking with their kids at Disneyland), and I'd be his stalwart helpmate. I'd drive him to various ERs while he barfed into garbage bags, sit in surgical waiting rooms listening to the life stories of people I'd never see again, and call concerned friends and family members as soon as I got home. To the outside world, I was a saint—my mother's daughter. In private, I was cursing Michael for leaving me over and over again, resenting him for disrupting my work routine, hating him for depriving me of the kind of normalcy I was sure every other couple was enjoying.

Who was this person? One minute he was the handsome, gentle man I'd married; the next he was pumped up with steroids, bloated and moonfaced, screaming obscenities, and punching walls. One minute I was praying he wouldn't die; the next I was hoping he would. He was the perennial patient, but—little did I know—his illness and my conflicted feelings were making me sick.

Okay, why is she telling us all this, you're probably asking yourself if you've bothered to read this far? Or, perhaps, you're asking: Does the world really need yet another book in support of the noble, compassionate, utterly frazzled people who care for loved ones with health problems? Don't we already have dozens of titles on the subject—elegiac illness memoirs, thought-provoking treatises on death and dying, imposing reference volumes full of resources, not to mention perky self-help manuals that teach us how to clip our elderly, dementia-impaired parents' toenails? And aren't there a million websites and blogs that offer more advice than a caregiver could possibly have time to digest?

All very valid questions, and I'd be asking them myself.

So here's why I wrote this book despite all the others out there:

    ✳   I wanted to add my two cents, chime into the conversation, move off the sidelines, because the subject is too important for me to remain a detached observer.

* I wanted to share my adventures in caregiving—what's worked for me as well as the mistakes I've made—and enlist experts to show me (and you) how we can do things better.

* I wanted to help all of us take care of ourselves so we're able to take care of those we love—from how to get the proper exercise to how to get a decent night's sleep. And, trust me, I'm not coming at this from some preachy, soap-boxy point of view. I used to roll my eyes at all the well-meaning people who kept telling me to stop neglecting my own health—until I could no longer ignore what was happening inside my body. I ended up going from caregiver to caregivee, thanks to several skin cancer surgeries and a hysterectomy, but I was lucky to have a spouse who was eager to switch places and take care of me for a change.

* I wanted to express (and encourage you to express) the emotions we all have when caring for a loved one but are often too guilt-ridden, fearful, or embarrassed to say what's really on our minds.

* I wanted to reach out to other caregivers, including a few whose names you'll recognize from movies, television, and publishing, and let them vent or offer inspiration or serve up a helpful tip or two. I've never joined a support group in all the years I've been a caregiver, so talking to them during the interviews they

were generous enough to give has allowed me to feel as if I've started a little group of my own.

* I wanted to ask, "Is this normal?" in a variety of care-giving situations—and get the answers. Is it normal to be intimidated by doctors, to be flummoxed by the health-care system, to be mad at your sister, to wish you could rewind your life? How do we know what's normal unless we have specialists to tell us? This book has specialists.

* I wanted you to laugh. No surprise there if you've ever read any of my novels, which are comedies and demon-strate my firm belief that humor gets us through even the bleakest hours. That's where the title of this book comes from: the part of me that makes jokes. Whenever Michael would be wheeled into the operating room and one of the surgical nurses would stop the gurney just before it arrived at those scary-looking double doors, turn to me and advise, "Sorry, but you'll have to say your goodbyes here," a giant lump would form in my throat, tears would prick at my eyes, and instead of grabbing her by the collar of her blue scrubs and screech-ing, "No! Wait! Please don't take my husband away!" I'd lower my face close to Michael's, give him a kiss on the mouth, and crack, "You'd better not die or I'll kill you." He'd laugh and so would the nurse, and then off he'd go.

✳ I wanted to give you a book that would be a pal for life, without judgment, without strings, without pre-existing conditions—a book that you could pick up and read at any point, on any page, and find something useful. In other words, I wanted to be the cheery, knowledgeable companion I wish I'd had when I was sitting in Michael's hospital rooms, sliding off those uncomfortable chairs, smelling hospital smells, hearing hospital sounds, feeling hopeless and alone and sorry for myself. There's a chapter coming up about friendship—how people often drift away when a family member has a chronic or progressive illness. This book won't drift away. It won't stop calling or forget to ask how things are or say, "We must get together," and then never follow up. It will be there for you whenever and wherever you need it.

Sound like a plan? Good.

CHAPTER 1

What Is a Caregiver Anyway?

- - - - - - - - - - - - - -

"I used to be cute before all this caregiving. Now I look like I'm a hundred."

—BARBARA BLANK, caregiver

Here's a little quiz. If you answer yes to any of the following questions, you're officially a caregiver and I salute you. Well, maybe a salute doesn't do us justice; we should probably have a secret handshake—something cool where we slide our palms together, grab hold of our thumbs, and finish up with a fist bump.

* Have you ever said the words "I can't take it anymore?" More than once, in fact?

* Have you fantasized about flying to Fiji—by yourself?

* Have you spent an inordinate amount of time engaged in imaginary conversations with doctors in which you ask all the things you intended to ask but didn't?

* Have you fallen asleep at your desk, snapped at someone in a supermarket checkout line, or cried in the bathroom?

＊ Have you had the thought: "I should be getting paid for this?"

＊ Have you looked in the mirror and wondered if you've always had those craters under your eyes?

＊ Have you jumped when the phone rang and actually felt relieved when it was a telemarketer?

＊ Have you worn enough Purell to disinfect an entire third world country?

＊ Have you said about a hospital cafeteria: "Why are the trays always wet?" Or: "That chicken gumbo wasn't as bad as it looked." Or: "Does Melba toast still have to taste like cardboard after all these years?"

＊ Have you worked up a nice, simmering resentment toward a sister or brother who tends to leave all the heavy lifting to you? Or, conversely, have you been weighted down by guilt because you aren't the daughter/son who lives in the same town as Mom or Dad?

＊ Have you wondered why the patient in the bed or room next door to your beloved always has the TV on too loud, not to mention tuned to *The Price Is Right?*

＊ Have you gotten tired of people telling you to "hang in there"?

＊ Has your heart swelled with affection for a nurse or an aide who acknowledged your existence?

＊ Have you made a morning vow to get more exercise— only to slip into bed at night and say hopefully, "Maybe tomorrow"?

＊ Has your upper lip ever started twitching for no apparent reason?

* Have you told yourself it's okay to eat that entire bag of Doritos Nacho Cheese Flavored Tortilla Chips in one sitting because you've "earned it"?

* Are you on a first-name basis with the guy at the pharmacy?

* Do you yearn for the days when your loved one was healthy enough to piss you off?

So tell me: How'd you do on the quiz? Did anything on the list ring a bell? At least one thing?

I bet you're nodding. The point I'd like to make here is that caregivers—no matter what our backgrounds and circumstances—have a lot in common. I find that very comforting. I like that we're all in this together. I feel heartened that, while we all want what's best for our loved ones, would move mountains on their behalf, and feel tremendously grateful for the time we're able to spend getting to know them in ways we'd never experience if they weren't sick, we can still say without the slightest hesitation, "Man, is this the pits or what?"

So yes, caregivers share a mindset. On the other hand, we come in all shapes and sizes and there's no one single definition; the term is and should be broad.

Some people care for a spouse or life partner.

Some people care for a child.

Some people care for a dear friend or neighbor.

Some people care for an elderly parent or relative.

Some people are on the scene 24/7 with sole responsibility for care.

Some people are on the scene with assistance from a professional companion or health-care worker.

Some people are long-distance caregivers who do what they can from afar.

Some people care for a parent *and* children simultaneously and are part of the so-called "sandwich generation."

Some people are pressed into service in fits and starts, the result of the patient's flare-ups during the course of a chronic illness.

Some people are called upon to serve suddenly and dramatically, following an accident or unexpected crisis.

Some people are simply Good Samaritans who want to help whenever there is a need.

Some people are taking care of someone with a terminal illness.

Some people are riding out a medical condition that will improve over time.

There's no story that's "worse" than another; caregiving is not a competitive sport. I like that part too—that we don't have to play, "Can you top this?" We each appreciate what the other is going through.

There are many ways to be a caregiver, in other words, and there are many of us who fill the role—65 million of us in the United States alone, according to the National Family Caregivers Association, which means that 29 percent of the adult population is walking around stretched and pulled in all directions. I'm glad there's a name for us now, because there was a time when it wasn't even in the lexicon.

Take my mother, for instance. My father died of brain cancer when I was six, but what I remember most about my early years was how normal they seemed in some ways. My mother got me and my sister off to school on time, arranged our play dates with friends, and sent us to summer camp, where we learned how to make potholders and ashtrays and whistle lanyards—all while my father suffered one medical crisis after another. She "juggled well" is what people said about her, since this was the 1950s, when there were euphemisms for just about every sort of unpleasantness.

And then he died and she fell apart. She became convinced that she, too, had a brain tumor, only to be told by each doctor she consulted that she was exhausted from years of looking after my father. She was suffering from a classic case of "caregiver burnout," another term nobody used back in the day.

Three years later, she met and eventually married my step-father, a widower with four kids. He was the picture of health—a strapping, broad-shouldered former collegiate track-and-field star who happened to have epilepsy. At first there were merely the seizure-related mishaps—a broken jaw, a cracked rib, reactions to medications. Then came more serious complications and a long, steady decline. My mother remained in caregiver mode through it all—even as she raised four stepchildren along with my sister and me and worked part time as a professor of Greek and Latin. After he died, she felt lost again. Caregiving had been her "job," her purpose. She was almost too good at juggling.

There was no appropriate term for me either when Michael was hospitalized with an intestinal obstruction in the early '90s—the first such episode since we'd been together.

"Are you his wife?" asked the nurses, the doctors, the insurance lady, even the guy who came to draw his blood.

"Girlfriend," I'd tell them all and wait for The Look. I was the only one there, the only one who stuck around, the only one who contacted his siblings and brought him his boating magazines and helped him figure out how to work the arcane TV remote—and yet "girlfriend" didn't cut it, judging by their air of dismissal. I might as well have said I was a hooker he'd picked up off the street. (Important note: The role of girlfriend is perfectly respectable nowadays and you can be thoroughly in charge of your loved one's care—provided you are so designated in a power of attorney document.)

The fact that I lacked a suitable title really rattled cages when I appeared at the hospital outside of permitted visiting hours. Girlfriends weren't considered immediate family back then, so there were times when I had to muscle my way in.

"What are you doing here?" a nurse asked when I showed up in Michael's room one morning before seven.

"Visiting the patient," I said.

"Are you his wife?"

"No."

"Sister?"

"Nope."

"Then you shouldn't be here."

"Let me ask you something," I said, trying to remain calm and polite. "Do you want him pressing the 'call' button every six seconds? Or would it make your life easier if I handled the simple chores?"

She scowled, put her hands on her ample hips. She was a boxy woman with a not-so-faint-mustache, and I could easily picture her serving as a prison warden. "Rules are rules, and—"

"Let me ask you something else," I interrupted, figuring a new tactic was in order. "Have you ever been in love?"

"Excuse me?"

"In love. You know."

Her expression softened. "As a matter of fact, I'm getting married in three months."

"Congratulations!" I said, reaching for her hand and pumping it vigorously. "Have you picked out your dress?"

Well, that did it. Get a woman talking about her wedding and she forgets to be mad at you.

She described the dress, the bridesmaids' dresses, the flowers, the cake, *blah blah blah*. She was my new best friend and by the time she left I could have shown up at the crack of dawn and it would have been okay.

Not that I was always so charming. During that same hospital stint, I had asked Michael if he'd be okay without me for a day. The two-hour drive between Connecticut and Manhattan was wearing me down and I was desperate to get back to the novel I was writing, not to mention have some quiet time to myself. He said he understood and I was grateful.

About two hours into my solitude, I called him to check in.

"Everything okay there?" I asked.

"I'm really cold," said Michael, his voice tremulous, near tears.

"What do you mean, 'You're really cold'?" I said, assuming he was just "in a mood." He was on high doses of medication, including prednisone, and his emotions were all over the place.

"I can't get anyone to give me a blanket and it's freezing in here. I pressed the call button for the nurses, but no one will help me."

It's a cliché to write, "Smoke came out of my ears," but that's exactly what I felt like when he said that: mad enough to breathe fire. Michael is the antithesis of a complainer; he could be bleeding from his eyeballs and he'd tell you he was fine.

"I'll be right there," I said.

I made it to the city in record time. I parked near the hospital, marched inside, rode up in the elevator to Michael's room, and found him in bed with his pathetic blue windbreaker draped over his shivering body. Oh, and he was right about the temperature: it was a meat locker in there.

"Give me a sec," I told him and stomped into the hall to the nurses' station. Have you seen the movie *Terms of Endearment?* If so, remember when Shirley MacLaine had a meltdown, demanding that somebody give Debra Winger her pain meds? Well, I pulled a Shirley.

"*Can somebody give my boyfriend a goddamn blanket?*" I yelled, as a handful of nurses stared at me. They looked frightened. I felt ashamed.

"I'm sorry." I began again, less noisily this time. "I realize you're busy and this isn't on the level of a Code Blue, but I shouldn't have to drive two hours to ask one of you to stop ignoring your patient, who has asked several times for a blanket and not gotten one."

Michael got a blanket. Actually, he got three blankets. And more ice chips for his dry mouth, a fresh box of tissues, and a lot of plumping of pillows and adjusting of his bed.

I wasn't proud of my tone or my language or of having to raise my voice, but there are times when you can't help yourself if you're a caregiver. Which is what, even though the term wasn't in widespread usage yet, is exactly what I was.

Over the course of writing this book, I've talked to other caregivers whose specific experiences are very different from my own but whose emotions, thoughts, and knack for finding humor in even the grimmest circumstances have mirrored mine. I think of them now as members of the book's Greek chorus—and as my support group. Let me introduce them.

➤ **Yudi Bennett, CA:** A former award-winning assistant director in Hollywood whose credits include *Kramer vs. Kramer* and *Broadcast News*, Yudi is now a single mother and caregiver to her autistic son after having lost her husband to lymphoma.

➤ **Barbara Blank, FL:** Barbara is the primary caregiver for her ninety-six-year-old father, who lived with her before moving recently into a nearby seniors' community. Additionally, her husband suffers from hearing impairment and dementia.

➤ **Harriet Brown, NY:** A prolific writer and editor, Harriet chronicled her daughter's struggle with anorexia and her family's hands-on approach to caregiving in her critically acclaimed book *Brave Girl Eating*.

➤ **Linda Dano, CT:** The Daytime Emmy Award–winning actress, talk-show host, and designer of home accessories on QVC, Linda has seen her share of tragedy. She became the caregiver for her father (Alzheimer's), her mother (dementia), and her husband (lung cancer), and has toured extensively to raise awareness about caregiving and depression.

➤ **Jennifer DuBois, VA:** Jennifer took a leave of absence from her job as a corporate communications specialist to take charge of the care for her mother, who was dying of bone cancer.

➤ **Victor Garber, NY:** The versatile Emmy Award–winning star of stage and screen, Victor had two parents with Alzheimer's. He served as the primary caregiver for his mother while he was in L.A. garnering fans and accolades on the hit TV series *Alias*.

➤ **John Goodman, NY:** John's world changed when his wife of many years was suddenly diagnosed with the rarely understood Cushing's syndrome and he was catapulted into the role of caregiver.

➤ **Judy Hartnett, FL:** Judy was no stranger to challenges, having become the stepmother to her husband's young children when they were first married, but nothing prepared her for her role as his primary caregiver when he was diagnosed with MS.

➤ **Deborah Hutchison, CA:** A film producer and author, Deborah was called to action when her mother was diagnosed with Alzheimer's, and she became her mom's primary caregiver. She wrote the innovative and much-needed book *Put It in Writing: Creating Agreements Between Family and Friends*, which includes the agreement "Caring for Our Aging Parents."

➤ **Michael Lindenmayer, IL:** Michael took a year's sabbatical from his business ventures to help his worn-out parents care for his elderly grandfather. After experiencing the challenges caregivers face, he created the Caregiver Relief Fund, which provides four hours of respite to deserving applicants.

➤ **Suzanne Mintz, MD:** The diagnosis of her husband's MS and her experiences caring for him motivated Suzanne to cofound a newsletter for caregivers that eventually grew into the National Family Caregivers Association (NFCA), one of the nation's go-to resources for education, support, and advocacy.

➤ **Jeanne Phillips, CA:** Jeanne took over the writing of Dear Abby, the world's most widely syndicated column, when her mother, Pauline Phillips, also known as Abigail Van Buren, was diagnosed with Alzheimer's. She reaches out personally to those who write to the column asking for help with an Alzheimer's patient.

➤ **Suzanne Preisler, NY:** When her younger sister was diagnosed with ovarian cancer, Suzanne became her caregiver and most ardent champion, seeing her through a successful ten-year battle. She was called upon again when she learned that her mother had pancreatic cancer.

➤ **Karen Prince, CA:** Karen's husband suffered a massive stroke in his forties. Despite his inability to walk or talk, she not only took care of him but also moved them both across the country to California, where they lived for years until he succumbed to lung cancer.

➤ **April Rudin, NJ:** A busy mother of two children, April nevertheless shared primary caregiving responsibilities with her sister for their beloved grandmother, who lived 3,000 miles away and had Alzheimer's. She made frequent trips across the country to handle all medical issues.

➤ **Harold Schwartz, FL:** Harold's son was in the prime of his life when he was diagnosed with ALS. Harold handled the caregiving on weekends and marveled at how his son never lost hope. He then cared for his wife, who suffered from Parkinson's.

➤ **Toni Sherman, CA:** When her daughter contracted a serious foot infection, Toni took care not only of her child but also of her child's children. Soon after, Toni's mother received a diagnosis of peritoneal cancer, and her caregiving duties doubled.

➤ **John Shore, CA:** Christian blogger, humorist, and author of *Penguins, Pain and the Whole Shebang*, John had a turbulent relationship with his father, from whom he was estranged. But that didn't stop him from moving into his dad's house and assuming the role of caregiver when his father needed help after a stroke.

➤ **Diane Sylvester, Cissy Ross, Jackie Walsh, and Cecilia Johnston, CA:** This group of remarkable women met while their mothers (and Cecilia's father) were all residents of the Samarkand, a seniors' community in Santa Barbara, and bonded over their caregiving experiences. Diane's mother suffered from depression and dementia. Cissy's mother lost her ability to speak after a series of neurological problems. Jackie's mother had severe macular degeneration, fell and broke her hip, and suffered a stroke. Cecilia's mother, the only surviving mom of the four, has Alzheimer's.

Every member of my new support group will be offering up some of what they've felt, thought, and learned over the years since they were tagged with the responsibility of caring for a loved one. They are wise, resourceful, funny, and courageous, and have managed to find silver linings in their darkest moments. I salute them—and give them a fist bump.

CHAPTER 2

Navigating Past the Freak-Out

"You need your freak-outs. But you can't make decisions and freak out at the same time."

—TINA B. TESSINA, psychotherapist

Inevitably, there will be a phone call or a test result or an encounter with a grim-faced doctor—all conveying bad news about your loved one's health.

Not to state the obvious but bad news sucks. It plunges you into despair. It knocks out all sense of hope and possibility. It makes you wish it were all a crappy dream and you'd wake up and everything would be super-fabulous again. But here's what I have to say about bad news: although it will change your life in ways no one in their right mind would sign up for, it will also make you stronger. (Yes, that sentence borders on intellectual pabulum, but it's true.) Bad news will rehearse you, fortify you, steel you for the next time it comes along, and, just possibly, you'll do a better job of handling it. That's been the case with me, anyway.

As an inexperienced caregiver, I used to freak out whenever there was bad news about Michael. I let my emotions spill forth without any regard to how my behavior might affect him. I had no ability to stifle myself. I was operatic in my wailing, wildly irrational in my reactions—a certifiable drama queen.

The best way to get over being a hysteric when crises arise is to recognize that you're being a hysteric, and I wasn't able to do that early in my relationship with Michael.

Take the time his gastroenterologist punctured his colon during a colonoscopy: I had gone with him to the doctor's office in Manhattan to wait during the procedure and take him home afterward. What did I know from colonoscopies back then? This was pre-*Today* show Katie Couric. I'd never heard of people having a TV camera jammed up their derriere.

"Routine thing to check for polyps," Michael told me.

If you say so, I thought. *I'll bring a book and sit there for twenty minutes.*

An hour later, Michael emerged looking like death. I'd describe his color as a shade somewhere between milk and the GEICO lizard.

"What's wrong?" I said as I helped him out the door.

"I'm in a lot of pain," he said, clutching his abdomen.

We drove home to Connecticut. His pain worsened. He called the doctor. The result? Back to the city—and to the hospital.

"You told me it was a routine procedure!" I said accusingly, as if Michael had betrayed me with all his nonchalance. I had fallen in love with him for many reasons, one of which was his low-key, soft-spoken manner. Now, that very same low-keyness was confusing me.

"It's routine if you don't have Crohn's," he clarified. "I had fifteen years of prednisone therapy, which can cause a thinning of the intestines."

He was so sweet, so forgiving. I, on the other hand, was poised to stab the doctor in the testicles.

The plan was to put Michael on antibiotics and "wait and see."

"Wait and see what?" I said too loudly into the phone when the God of Gastroenterology called Michael's hospital room. That's how we referred to him, because he was such a big shot in his field. Sometimes we shortened the nickname to GOG.

"See if the puncture will heal on its own," said the GOG.

"What if it doesn't?" I asked. The word "puncture" sounded so violent, so destructive. And we were talking about one of Michael's vital organs, after all.

"Then we'll just do an ileostomy," he said.

I blinked a few times, making sure I'd heard him correctly. I had no idea what he was talking about, but anything ending in *ostomy* couldn't be good, could it?

"We make an incision through the abdominal wall into the ileum," he went on, "so that waste can be discharged through the body without passing through the colon, enabling it to rest."

"Are you suggesting surgery?" I said, my anxiety rising. How had a run-of-the-mill colonoscopy turned into something so scary?

"We bring the ileum to the surface of the abdomen, creating a stoma."

"Okay, I need you to speak English now."

He sighed, as if he couldn't believe he'd been dragged into a conversation with someone so hopelessly uninformed. "The ileum is the small intestine and a stoma is an opening. We attach a plastic bag to the stoma in order to catch the waste."

"*A plastic bag?*"

I didn't even try not to go nuts. In that moment I was incapable of processing the bulletin that my boyfriend, the man I was going to marry, was about to live his life wearing a Hefty CinchSak attached to his stomach.

"It'll be temporary," said the GOG in a way that was probably intended to reassure me. "Just three months—until the colon is completely healed and functioning."

I couldn't speak. I had started to cry.

"And today's ostomy bags are very user-friendly," he continued. "They come in two kinds: one has a Velcro-type closure that allows the waste to be emptied into the toilet; the other is close-ended and must be replaced each time it's full, like a vacuum cleaner bag. Both come with charcoal-filtered vents so that when the patient has gas, the pouches will inflate, which prevents ballooning, particularly at night. As for leakage, it can be a problem, but the newer products do a much better job of containing the fecal matter. Any more questions?"

Yeah, like what time is the first plane out of here?

I mean come on. I was in shock. I realize that there are many people living active, extremely productive lives in spite of wearing a bag, but the notion was just not within my frame of reference. I kept picturing Jon Voight in the movie *Coming Home.* Remember the scene in the beginning when his bag of urine explodes all over the place with Jane Fonda looking on? And then there were the images dancing around in my head of the wedding Michael and I were planning—a wedding that could easily turn into a nightmare. We would be standing up at the altar, dressed in white, holding hands, gazing adoringly into each other's eyes, about to say our vows in front of our family and friends, when suddenly he would have "leakage." Oh, God.

"I can't believe this," I said between sobs. "I just can't."

"I don't know why you're so upset," said the doctor. "It's not that big a deal."

"It is so!" I said hotly and proceeded to sob some more. "You just don't understand!"

Yes, I was a hysteric on that occasion, and it helped no one. The good news is that Michael's colon healed quickly, requiring none of the measures the doctor had described so winningly. He was out of the hospital within days and we were married on a crisp fall afternoon in Connecticut without leakage or seepage or any other discharging of bodily fluids.

Fast forward six years, during which there had been numerous trips to the ER as a result of Michael's Crohn's. I had become more and more competent in my caregiving skills once I finally came to terms with the fact that *my* fears, *my* disappointments, *my* tears were not doing him any favors. He needed me and I needed to be fully in control—for him.

We had moved to South Florida by this time and he was recovering at home after surgery for an intestinal blockage. At five a.m., he woke me, holding his gut, and said, "Can you take me to the hospital—now?"

I was still groggy, but there was no mistaking that his incision had sprung a leak; something was definitely and disgustingly oozing from between the stitches.

I threw on some clothes, bundled Michael up in a raincoat, and off we went to the hospital. The surgeon on call was practically out the door, having ended his shift, and didn't look too pleased to have to deal with one more case. He was very preppy in his Ralph Lauren shirt, khakis, and tasseled loafers, and he announced that he had an early tee time to get to.

"Your husband has an infection," he told me as we stood over the patient in a little cubicle in the ER. "I need to go in, clean it out, and sew him up."

"So you'll take him to surgery," I said. It wasn't a question.

He glanced at his watch and shook his head. "We'll do it right here. It'll be quicker."

The old me would have exploded. This guy was in such a hurry to chase a little white ball around a golf course? But he was the one in charge and he had already called for a nurse to assist and we were rolling. Not that he bothered to put on scrubs or a lab coat. He was going ahead in his Polo best. "Is it okay if I stay?" I asked.

He laughed. "If you don't faint at the sight of a man's belly being filleted."

"I can take it if you can," I said in what I thought was a very snappy retort. I had no idea if I could take it, but we were about to find out.

I grabbed Michael's hand and squeezed it as the surgeon began to wield his scalpel. Oh, did I mention that the morphine drip in the IV hadn't kicked in yet and that my husband was screaming his lungs out—all because Tiger Woods was on the clock?

"Can't you wait for his pain medicine to work?" I said, hating to see Michael in such agony.

"He'll be fine," said Tiger as he went about his business.

His "business," of course, was to operate on Michael's abdomen, and he seemed to be doing it skillfully. How do I know? I watched every gory second of the surgery. That's right. I stared down into my beloved's gaping wound without flinching, fainting, or hurling. I just kept squeezing his hand, whispering that everything would be all right, and ticking off all the fun things we'd do when he was feeling better.

At one surreal point, I sort of stepped outside of my body and said to myself, "Who are you and what have you done with Jane?"

I guess what I'm saying is that the more you stare into the abyss, the easier it gets. Okay, not "easier." It's never easy. But what's the choice? You have to learn to get your act together—for everybody's sake.

I asked a few of my fellow caregivers how they handled the test result/phone call/horrendous diagnosis when they were confronted with it. As you can see, freaking out even a little is perfectly natural, normal, and healthy, and you'd have to be a complete blockhead not to feel like doing it.

➤ **Yudi Bennett:** "At age two and a half, my son Noah suddenly stopped talking. He went from a kid who was babbling and said, 'Mom' to a kid who could only say, '*Mmm.*' We became very alarmed and took him to a speech therapist who said, 'He's definitely not autistic. He just has a language delay.' It took five doctors until we got one we could trust because people just weren't trained in those days and pediatricians didn't have a clue.

"Finally he was diagnosed by a really wonderful psychologist. I sat down and cried for two weeks. My first thought was, who will take care of him when I'm not around? I was not a young mom at forty-four. I also remembered how my husband, Bob, and I would kid around when I was pregnant about where our child would go to college, what he'd be when he grew up, would he have my art genes or Bob's literary genes. You do a lot of fantasizing. After we got the diagnosis I kept saying, 'Nothing is going to be the way we thought it was. Everything has changed.' And I was right.

"It was different with Bob's lymphoma. He went in for surgery to remove his spleen, because they knew he had tumors but they didn't know what kind. I was sitting in the waiting room and doctors were coming out and talking to people. But the doctor who operated on Bob took me into a private room. That's when I knew the tumors were malignant and my heart sank. We were then referred to an oncologist who said, 'This type of cancer is very aggressive but eighty percent of the time it's curable with chemotherapy.' We thought eighty percent was great, so I didn't cry for two weeks this time. I hoped the cancer would have a beginning, a middle, and an end, unlike Noah's special needs, which is a lifelong thing."

➤ **Harriet Brown:** "Our daughter Kitty had just turned fourteen and she's our oldest so we didn't really know what it was going to look like to have a teenager. She was staying away from dessert and she was an athlete, doing gymnastics and exercising a lot. Within that context it looked positive to us. But I had been worried about her being a little too thin. She never really lost a bunch of weight at once. It was more that she didn't gain weight when she should have. And then I started to notice behaviors around eating and pretty much knew it had to be anorexia at that point. Still, it took a while for her to be diagnosed and that was partly my fault. I think if I had told the doctors, 'We really need to see you right now,' they would have gotten us in sooner. It was sort of like, 'I don't really want to see this. *La la la.* Put my fingers in my ears.'

"I think all families are in denial at first. As parents you just don't want it to be true. By the time we did go to the doctor for the diagnosis, we all pretty much knew it. I didn't freak out because I was fairly ignorant about eating disorders. I figured, well, here we are. We loved our doctor. She was great. But I started to panic when I realized she didn't have any real help for us. Nobody had any real, solid, proven help for us. I realized at a certain point, *My God. We're in this kind of on our own.* She told me flat out, 'I've never had a kid this sick before.' She was out there looking for information and we were out there looking for information, and nobody was driving the bus. That was very scary."

➤ **Linda Dano:** "I had no idea my father had Alzheimer's—none. My husband, Frank, and I had decided my parents would come and live with us. Since I was working on *Another World*, Frank went to California to bring them to New York. My father and mother got on that plane and my father went crazy. He punched

Frank in the face, cut open his lip. Within three days I started living a Stephen King story.

"I didn't know it at the time, but if you move an Alzheimer's patient, they fall off the end of the earth. My father tore the apartment apart. He choked my mother. He fell. We got him to the emergency room at Mount Sinai and they had to put him in restraints. Now this was my John Wayne, and yet there he lay— wrestling and fighting and yelling. It went downhill from there. He was admitted into the psych ward. He was there for a week and a half and then stopped eating. I was told he needed a feeding tube. They kept saying I'd be a bad daughter if I let him go that way. I didn't know what to do and my mother had turned the whole thing over to me, so I was legally in charge. I gave him the feeding tube. Still, no one ever said he had Alzheimer's.

"He finally got diagnosed because I had done a talk show and one of the guests was a Dr. Butler, head of geriatrics at Mount Sinai. One night I sat up in bed and said, 'Frank! Let's call Dr. Butler.' And we did. The next morning I met him at Mount Sinai and he said, 'Your father has Alzheimer's,' and he explained what it was. I freaked out because I would never ever have given him the feeding tube if I'd known.

"A few years after he died, my mother changed. There was a distance about her. She'd had tiny strokes over the years, but they would happen and go away. This was different. She was walking and talking but she wasn't making a lot of sense. We ran all these tests and she had dementia, not Alzheimer's. I was completely in control this time. I knew what to do to take care of her.

"Then came Frank's diagnosis. I had stopped working and had promised I would go to Normandy with him. I was free. We had money. We were going to travel. And it all came crashing down. It started with laryngitis. He had a CAT scan and they found this mass right next to his aorta. I started to cry. I was so afraid. When somebody says to you, 'Your husband has stage four lung cancer,' you know what that means unless you're a moron. He was everything to me. He filled every little nook and cranny of my life. My world spun in front of me."

➤ **Jennifer DuBois:** "My mom started out with some low back pain and she thought it was sciatica. She went to the doctor and they had her do physical therapy for six weeks and nothing was helping. Finally they sent her in for an MRI. That's when they looked at her lower back and said, 'This doesn't look good.' They knew they weren't dealing with simple sciatica but something much worse. They went in and did a bone biopsy. That's when they found the cancer in her bones, which had metastasized from somewhere else; they never found the original site, but they could tell it was consistent with lung cancer that had metastasized.

"It was my father who called me with the diagnosis. I was at the Hotel Sofitel in Miami. Hurricane Katrina was heading our way and we had no electricity. I was on storm duty for the company I worked for. My dad called my cell phone and told me the news, and I was in shock. My mother was the picture of health at sixty-five. She worked out. She ate right. It just didn't sink in, and I didn't realize it was terminal. It took a couple of days for me to really understand, for it to become real."

➤ **Victor Garber:** "My mother was living in Los Angeles on her own in a one-bedroom apartment in West Hollywood. When I got a job on *Alias*, I arrived from New York and she was okay. She was functioning. I wasn't aware of any problems. She and my father had been divorced for years and she was basically living week-to-week, off Social Security, and working part time.

"One day she said, 'I don't think I can do this job for much longer.' I said, 'Why?' She said, 'I'm starting to forget things and I had a very embarrassing day.' She had missed an appointment and misplaced something and she was very, very upset. I said, 'Well, Mom, if it's too much you'll find something less stressful and don't worry about it.' But I could tell that something was happening. There was a sign, a red flag. So she left that job and for the next year or so it got to the point where she couldn't work.

"She was seeing a therapist, a very nice guy, and one day we went to see him together because by that time I knew something was really off. The therapist said to her, 'You exhibit all the signs of Alzheimer's.' Like always, she was slightly in denial and didn't really believe it. She said, 'Oh? Really?' I knew it was the beginning of a terrible journey."

➤ **Judy Hartnett:** "My husband, Paul, was diagnosed with MS thirteen or fourteen years ago. At first we thought he was just klutzy; he couldn't walk with you on a sidewalk without literally bumping into you. Then his gait got worse. He started by asking the internist about it at his annual checkup and the internist said, 'Maybe you have a drug or alcohol problem.' Paul was like, 'Thanks a lot, but I'm pretty sure I'd know if I had one.' The next doctor sent him to a specialist who checked for a mini-stroke. He didn't have anything like that. Other doctors said, 'Eat better. Try this pill. Brush your teeth more.' No one said anything smart—just dumb feedback.

"It was a long, slow road to a definitive diagnosis. Finally, a neurologist sent us to the University of Miami. The doctor asked Paul if he could walk back into the office so he could observe him walking and doing other physical things. He never laid a hand on Paul. All he did was watch. When he was finished watching, he said to Paul, 'You have multiple sclerosis. There's no doubt in my mind.' I welled up and just sat absolutely silently.

"Paul turned into Barbara Walters and said, 'Okay. Let me just take some notes and we'll get started.' He was the kind of person you're supposed to bring with you when you're a patient. But I was numb. I thought, what the hell does this mean? Where is this going? Someone's going to completely depend on me? No one likes when their parents get sick, but you kind of expect it as they age. You don't expect it to be your husband. It was an overwhelmingly awful thing. Paul had always been fiercely independent—we both were—so I just didn't think we'd ever have to deal with this."

➤ **Jeanne Phillips:** "I worked with my mother for many years, long before she got Alzheimer's. As she began having problems, there would be glitches in the 'machinery' of producing the column. I would try to put out the little blazes that were popping up in front of me without realizing they could become a forest fire. It started with episodes of forgetfulness or disorganization. I couldn't accept the implications of what was happening. After 9/11, my husband

and I picked Mom up to take her out to dinner. Her housekeeper mentioned that Mom had been glued to the television set all day. When we started to talk at dinner about the horrific tragedy, she asked, 'What tragedy?' That was a shock.

"Then there was another time when I was talking with Mom about her twin sister. There had been a rift in the family for many years—it was well known. When I alluded to it, she asked me what I was talking about. Later, she had a personality breakdown. That's a strong word for it, but it was like a personality glitch. It was very traumatic to me, and at that point I understood that she was going to need more help than I was capable of giving. But you don't spend time beating your breast and saying, 'I can't believe this is happening.' You just deal with it. If there's something that comes up, you deal with it."

➤ **Suzanne Preisler:** "My sister got ovarian cancer when she was very young—only thirty—and it took awhile for it to be diagnosed. She started showing symptoms during the time she was trying to get pregnant. Her skin color didn't look right. She looked very drawn. She was bloated. It was amazing to me that the doctors she was seeing weren't picking up that there was something wrong with her. She began having very sharp pains in her abdomen. It turned out that she had a tumor the size of a grapefruit, so she had surgery to find out what was happening.

"By the time she was diagnosed, she was advanced. I started crying and kept crying for about two days. I had never lost anyone in my family. To think about losing the youngest one hit me like a ton of bricks. All we remembered was Gilda Radner and the terrible time she had, so I thought my sister was in store for the same thing. And since her husband wasn't up to being her primary caregiver, it was sort of left to me.

"With my mom, she and my sister-in-law lived in Florida and they used to go shopping once a week. One Thursday, my sister-in-law said to my mother, 'Your eyes don't look good.' When you have pancreatic cancer you get jaundice, so her eyes were a little yellow. My sister-in-law insisted that she go to the doctor, and they immediately put her in the hospital. At the time I didn't know anything about pancreatic cancer, so when my brother told me she was going to have surgery for it, I said, 'Should I come when she's out of the hospital so I can take care of her?' He said, 'No, you better come now.' It was terrible news."

➤ **Karen Prince:** "My husband, Andy, and I were shopping at Home Depot and the first thing that was strange was that he said he felt dizzy when he looked up but not when he looked down. We came home and I started preparing lunch and he was sitting at the table. All of a sudden he just keeled over on the floor. The first thing I thought of was a heart attack. But when I got down on the floor, the right side of his body was cold and the left side was not and there was just gibberish coming out of his mouth so I thought it was a stroke. I also thought it might be diabetes because he had that, but I knew his blood sugar wasn't low. I called 911.

"When the ambulance people came, they said, 'Well, it's probably his blood sugar.' I said, 'No, it isn't his blood sugar. He can't use his right side. He's speaking gibberish.' I was a nurse so I knew what I was talking about, but I was not calm. All my training was not helpful. When it's your own, it's different.

"The ambulance people got him on the gurney and out the door very fast. Then it was hours and hours of waiting at the hospital. I was thinking, what's going to happen down the line? Am I going to be able to keep the house? Finally the neurologist came out and told me Andy had definitely had a severe stroke. He couldn't swallow. He couldn't do anything. He was completely dependent. He was breathing on his own but that was it. When I went in to see him, I tried to keep it together because I didn't know if he understood anything at that point."

➤ **Harold Schwartz:** "My son Joseph was thirty-four and living in Washington, DC, when he was diagnosed with ALS. He had told my wife and me that sometimes his fingers felt a little cold, and I thought it was Raynaud's disease; I've known a lot of people with that. Also, he was a marathon runner in incredible condition, and he noticed his running was getting a little more difficult. We didn't think anything too much about it. Then he called and told us he had gone to numerous doctors and it sounded like he might have a brain tumor.

"It turns out it was Lou Gehrig's disease. I remember very clearly that he said, 'I do not feel like the luckiest man in the world.' I told my wife, 'Obviously Joseph's life has changed, but our lives have changed too.' I was devastated. The prognosis for Lou Gehrig's disease was two to five years. At one point, a neurologist told him he had two weeks to live. Joseph asked us to make funeral arrangements, go buy a plaque, pick out a casket, and we did that. But he lasted almost thirteen years with the most incredible spirit.

"It was about three years after he was diagnosed that my wife developed Parkinson's. She never had tremors. She had trouble writing. We sent her to a hand doctor. She called me at the office in tears and said, 'The doctor says I have Parkinson's.' I knew it was not a good disease, but I didn't think it would be as bad as it ultimately was. I guess I was naïve or stupid. It didn't hit me the way ALS did."

So yes, people have a hard time absorbing bad news, and there's plenty of it to go around. Not a day goes by that I don't hear about this one's son who got that terrible thing and this one's mother who got that terrible thing, and the truth is we're all going to get some terrible thing before it's all over unless we're, say, Betty White.

But this is not a bad news book and I am not a Debbie Downer. What I'm going to prove to anybody who sticks around long enough to read the whole thing is that the caregivers I spoke to managed not only to cope with bad news but also to experience genuine moments of happiness. They rolled up their sleeves and found ways to deal, as did I.

CHAPTER 3

Making Emergency Room Visits and Insanity Mutually Exclusive

- - - - - - - - - - - - -

"Most people are reasonable about the wait in the ER.
And those people who aren't? They could wait twenty minutes
and complain that they've waited too long."

—DR. ILENE BRENNER, emergency physician

I never watched *ER* when it was on TV—absolutely failed to notice the George Clooney phenomenon in its infancy. Not because I have anything against medical shows, mind you. In fact, as a kid I never missed an episode of *Dr. Kildare,* and I still remember the two-parter where Richard Chamberlain fell in love with Yvette Mimieux who had a seizure while surfing and died. I guess I was just busy having a life on Thursday nights when *ER* aired. What can I say?

The point is that I didn't come into this caregiving thing with any preconceived notions about emergency rooms, pro or con. But the longer I hung around Michael, the more I could tell that there was nothing TV-showish about them, nor did I ever spot a doctor who looked remotely like George Clooney. (I would have remembered, trust me.)

Michael and I were living in LA when he really gave our local ER a workout. Our place wasn't far from Cedars-Sinai Medical Center, luckily, but I can't even count how many trips we made there over a six-year period. I'd stuff him into the passenger seat of my Porsche, which we had dubbed "the ambulette," and off we'd go. He'd either be on the verge of an intestinal obstruction or actually have one, or sometimes he'd come down with creepy, inexplicable symptoms ranging from a freakishly swollen left cheek and neck (tooth gone bad) to dizzy spells that bordered on actual fainting (low hemoglobin due to internal bleeding). He gets infusions every six weeks of a genetically engineered drug called Remicade, which helps to manage his Crohn's but suppresses his immune system and allows for all sorts of secondary infections, most of which necessitate a trip to the ER.

Why didn't we just go to his doctor during normal business hours?

Please.

My husband never gets really sick unless it's a weekend or a holiday. I know I've mentioned this little quirk of his before, but it bears repeating. It's as if his body waits for Memorial Day, Labor Day, Christmas Day, and New Year's Day to fall apart.

At first, I'd view these jaunts to the ER as an adventure—an opportunity for me to be Wonder Woman, saving Michael from yet another threat from Planet Death. My adrenaline would start pumping and my brain would tick off all the plans I'd need to cancel, and I'd throw his insurance card, wallet, and one of his sailing magazines into a bag and whisk him away. I had superhuman strength. I walked and talked very fast. I was ready to do battle.

"You okay?" I'd ask him every six seconds, as I'd speed over to Cedars.

"Yeah," he'd say. "But could you please slow down? You're driving like a maniac."

"Oh. Sorry."

When we'd get to the ER, I would sit with him in the little triage room where the nurse asks what's wrong, what medications are you on, any allergies, do you smoke. Every time Michael would open his mouth, I would answer for him. I couldn't help myself. I was way too hyper to shut up.

When all the information was provided, we'd be instructed to join the 9,000 suffering individuals who'd been camped out in the waiting area for hours. They would cough on me. I would try not to breathe their germs. Many were not English speaking, since LA has a large population of Russians, Albanians, Persians, and others from lands I've never been to. There was a lot of moaning in foreign languages, in other words. There was also the homeless contingent that would be drunk and disorderly and get into fights with one another. One time a guy had to be Tasered by security right there in front of everybody. Another time three men came staggering in holding their faces, which were the color of canned tomatoes. I later learned that one of them was a severely depressed person who'd tried to jump off a bridge and kill himself; the other two were well-meaning police officers that had intervened by popping the suicidal guy with pepper spray. The wind had been blowing in the wrong direction, apparently, and all three of them got pepper sprayed, mostly in their eyes. I hate when that happens.

"Why aren't they taking you next?" I'd say to Michael after an hour or so. "That woman in the white turban just went back. We were here before she was."

"This isn't the DMV," he would remind me. "They take you according to the severity of your problem."

Eventually, they would come for Michael and I would insist on going back there with him and they would say no even after I played the "But I'm his wife and he needs me" card. After awhile, they'd come for me and I'd act very stoic while the doctor explained that Michael would have to be admitted into the hospital. He was always admitted. I had never once taken him to the ER and seen them send him away with a prescription and a "Good luck." After many, many hours I would go home alone and crash.

By the time we moved to Santa Barbara, where we live now, I had become far more blasé about Michael's trips to the ER. Well, not blasé, of course. Just less demonically possessed.

"I'm kind of busy," I'd say unless he had actually collapsed and stopped breathing. "Maybe you could drive yourself over there."

I'm kidding—sort of. There were times when his emergencies were only emergencies because he was Michael, the bubble boy who could pick up an infection if someone in the next town sneezed, and because they occurred, as usual, on a holiday.

I think I just came to dread the ER and tried to avoid it whenever possible. I was worn out by the endless waiting you have to do, the uncertainty of the diagnosis and treatment, the anticipation of losing Michael to yet another hospital stay and my having to be at home without him.

Still, given that the ER will be a part of my life as long as I'm married to a man who frequents them as often as most people frequent Starbucks, I figured I'd better educate myself about what really goes on there.

I sought out Ilene Brenner, MD, an ER doc at a major hospital in Atlanta. Ilene not only works twelve-hour shifts—at night, yet—but also has managed to write a couple of thrillers, a screenplay, and a nonfiction book called *How to Survive a Medical Malpractice Lawsuit*. Talk about multitasking. She was kind enough to let me barrage her with questions.

Jane: *Why is there such a long wait in the ER? Are you guys sitting around playing Scrabble on your iPads or something?*

Ilene: Last night I had a patient who had a heart attack and basically shut down the emergency department. When you have a patient who needs all your resources, the person with an earache is going to wait. That's why we have a triage system; the sickest patients come back first and everybody else experiences gridlock.

Jane: *Who qualifies as a "sickest patient"? Is there a pecking order?*

Ilene: My hospital uses the five-tier system. If you're in the first tier, you come in by ambulance. You're in cardiac arrest or you need a breathing tube or blood is pouring out of you, that kind of thing.

Jane: *Sounds reasonable.*

Ilene: The second-tier patient may or may not come by ambulance but has clear signs of having a heart attack or stroke—someone who needs immediate attention but is not quite dying.

Jane: *Not yet anyway.*

Ilene: The tier-three patients are the most common kind I have. They're not going to die but their symptoms are a concern. Like they have toe pain that's so bad their blood pressure is 200 systolic, which is very high.

Jane: *Toe pain gets you into the third tier?*

Ilene: Well, it's their blood pressure that's abnormal enough to get them back faster. And almost all patients with abdominal pain are level three because they usually need more complicated workups. The same goes for people with chest pain if they don't appear to be at death's door.

Jane: *So Michael must be a number three when he comes in. What's number four?*

Ilene: Almost everybody else: people with an earache, a sore throat, a runny nose, a mild cough.

Jane: *Level five must be for hypochondriacs.*

Ilene: We shouldn't even see level fives in the emergency department. They don't actually need medical care. They need suture removal or someone to eyeball something and reassure them that it's okay.

Jane: *When I go with Michael to the ER, I always try to be a good advocate for him. It gives me the sense that I'm not helpless.*

Ilene: So you bring his medical records?

Jane: *Um, no.*

Ilene: You should. My ideal caregiver is someone who has all the patient's records with them, plus a list of all their medical problems, all the names and phone numbers of their other doctors, and a detailed list of every medicine they're taking with the dosages, along with a copy of their EKG if they've had one.

Jane: *Oh, come on. Who keeps copies of that stuff?*

Ilene: You'd be surprised. I once had a patient who was visiting from India. He had everything with him and the information accelerated his workup dramatically and we got him the treatment he needed much faster. Until we have medical records that can be accessed as easily as money from an ATM, you as the caregiver are the one the doctor will look to for all the information.

Jane: *Got it. Is it kosher for caregivers to ask questions? I always have a million of them when I bring Michael to the ER, and I get the feeling the doctors find it annoying.*

Ilene: If you have questions, you should definitely ask them, but the doctor has a routine and if you interrupt it, the diagnosis could take twice as long.

Jane: *What's the routine?*

Ilene: I come into the room and ask, "What brings you here today?" And then the patient starts talking and based on what they say I ask follow-up questions. This continues until I get an idea of what's going on. Then I'll do the physical exam and pinpoint the problem. So wait until the tail end of the exam to ask your questions, which will give the doctor extra information about the patient that could be important.

Jane: *Why are some doctors such sourpusses? Seriously, some of them don't have much of a bedside manner.*

Ilene: Sometimes it's a personality thing. But often it's about how we handle stress. We don't mean to have "a tone," but maybe the previous patient set us off or the lab is delayed with a result or the CT scanner is down. Those kinds of things frustrate us and when we're frustrated we don't always mask it.

Jane: *Conversely, I can't stand it when the doctor tries to be friendly by shaking the patient's hand. I mean who knows where that hand has been?*

Ilene: The Japanese way of bowing is probably better. And you're right to try and protect your husband from germs. But I have to say that many, many caregivers don't do a very good job.

Jane: *Excuse me? You're knocking caregivers?*

Ilene: They try to do too much by keeping the patient at home, not having enough help, not putting Grandma in a facility. They're in denial. They're working so hard and doing everything they can, but they don't want her in a nursing home.

Jane: *Can you blame them?*

Ilene: No, but I see patients who are just not clean because they've been sitting in their own poop. Or they're not being adequately fed. The family members can't do it all, so the patient gets sicker as a result. They're unknowingly responsible for elder neglect and it's the last thing they want to happen. They may be saving the patient from the evil nursing home, but they're also trying to do more than they're capable of.

Jane: *What's the solution?*

Ilene: If you can access home-health nursing and have the resources for it, great. If not, do your research on nursing homes and find the best one. No matter what kind of nursing home it is, the more you visit, the better care your relative will get because the staff will know they're being watched. My dad used to bring cake to my grandmother's nursing home every time he came, so everybody loved him. A little food goes a long way with health-care people.

Jane: *What happens in the ER when there are numerous family members trying to make a life-and-death decision about Grandma's treatment? Do you listen to the one whose name is on the advance directive?*

Ilene: If there's no family member around, I go by the paperwork that's there; if there's a living will and it says the patient doesn't want extraordinary measures, we don't do extraordinary measures. If we have a patient who clearly should not be resuscitated and we have a phone number of a family member, we'll call and try to get an advance directive.

Jane: *What if the advance directive says one thing and the family member says another?*

Ilene: If the relative in control says to rip up the advance directive, we rip it up. I think it's wrong, because it goes against the patient's wishes, but that's how it works. Which is why each patient needs to be very careful about who gets power of attorney. Don't make it the son who never listened to you.

Jane: *What happens when a patient dies in the ER? I know as a doctor you must be used to it, but is it hard for you as a human being?*

Ilene: My mother died in an ER of a sudden heart attack when I was in med school, so I've been in the position of being the one to receive that horrible news. I'm fine with the natural passage of life, but dealing with the family members and their emotions triggers some sadness for me. I tear up 50 percent of the time.

Jane: *Do you have a script that you follow?*

Ilene: I do. I say, "This is what happened. We did everything we could. I'm sorry, but she died." I try to be as compassionate as possible, sit down with them, be at eye level, hold their hand, or touch their shoulder. One thing we were taught in residency was to make sure to use the words "died" and "dead." We do not say "pass away" or anything like that, because it allows family members to live in a state of denial. They have to acknowledge that their relative has died in order to move on. Beating around the bush is not compassionate.

Jane: *A very difficult job, I'm sure. Do you ever use humor to get through it?*

Ilene: Absolutely, even when a patient dies. Sometimes we'll get ten or fifteen family members in the room, and when you tell them what happened, they become so hysterical that we have to admit them into the hospital.

Jane: *And that's funny?*

Ilene: In a way, yeah. Our term for it is: "Stop, drop, and roll." They literally stop talking, do a belly flop onto the floor, and roll around crying. When you have multiple people doing it, it's crazy.

Jane: *You doctors are a laugh riot.*

Ilene: You have to understand that we've all faced that situation. Instead of crying about it, we laugh about it.

Jane: *Any final advice for caregivers?*

Ilene: Yes. I have a hard and fast rule about men: never let them come to the ER unaccompanied by a sister, a girlfriend, a wife, or a mother. Men are incapable of giving an appropriate history. They downplay everything. One man came in with an allergic reaction. I said, "Have you ever had an allergic reaction before?" "No." "Anything where you felt like your throat was closing up or you had itchy welts or even a light rash?" "Never." "You're sure?" "Positive." An hour later, his mother arrived and said, "Why aren't you doing this and this because he was in the ER a week ago with the exact same thing?" That's what men are like. They should never go to doctors' appointments on their own either.

Jane: *Amen. I tell Michael all the time, "Nagging wives save lives."*

Ilene: Oh, one more thing. Can you guess the most dangerous day to go to the hospital?

Jane: *Christmas Day—Michael's favorite time to get sick.*

Ilene: No. It's July 1—the day all the doctors and residents and medical students get promoted to the next level. Everybody is starting a new role and they're all clueless.

Jane: *Good to know. So Christmas Day isn't so bad after all.*

Ilene: Actually, it's the second most dangerous day. People want off. Nurses call in sick. The doctors who are working have worked many, many days in a row and are overtired. And the patients are at their most acute. Try to avoid that day.

Jane: *Fat chance.*

CHAPTER 4

Doctors—Can't Live with 'Em, Can't Live Without 'Em

- - - - - - - - - - - - -

"When you meet a doctor, interview him. 'Can you do this, this and this?' If he can't, you say, 'Sorry. Nice to meet you, but I don't think you fit what I'm looking for.' Just being able to say that changes things. When you're out picking and choosing, you need to have the power to say no instead of being stuck with someone and being angry and resentful."
—NEAL MAZER, psychiatrist

As the caregiver of a spouse who has had enough doctors over the years to populate an entire city, I can honestly say I've met them all—the nice ones, the mean ones, the hip ones, the nerdy ones, the talented ones, the clueless ones, the ones who take the time to listen, the ones who blow you off without a backward glance, the ones who deserve our undying gratitude, the ones who deserve to have their medical license revoked.

Who doesn't have doctor stories? Here are a few of mine:

* Michael was scheduled to undergo a procedure with a doctor who showed up forty-five minutes late and who said, without a trace of embarrassment or apology, "I overslept."

✳ I was in Michael's hospital room one morning and the doctor's prescription pad fell out of his pocket onto the floor. He nodded at me to pick it up for him. (I did not.)

✳ Michael was only fourteen when he was diagnosed with Crohn's. He and his bewildered mother were in the doctor's office.

The doctor to his mother: "Your son has terminal ileitis."

His mother: "Terminal? He's going to die?"

The doctor (with attitude): "No, not *that* kind of 'terminal.' Here. You can read about it in this."

At which point he reached for a huge medical textbook and flung it across the room at her.

✳ Michael went for a first appointment with a new primary-care physician, a young woman who was in our network of providers. He had just had a section of his nose removed due to melanoma surgery and was heavily bandaged. She not only did not look up from her notes to ask him what had happened to his nose, but she began by saying he needed to "make it quick" because she had to get home before her babysitter left.

✳ Michael was in excruciating pain for what he knew (from experience) to be a kidney stone. He was referred to a urologist who tested him and found no evidence of any stone. Michael assured him he had a stone, as small and undetectable as it might be, and asked for pain medication. The doctor refused, telling Michael he was probably an addict who was only there to score some Vicodin. The next day Michael passed the stone, put it in an empty pill bottle, and dropped it off at the doctor's office with a note that said, "Here's a present for you. Thanks for all your help."

Not that there haven't been wonderful, positive doctor stories; Michael wouldn't be alive if not for caring professionals and their expertise. Here are some examples:

* Michael's first surgeon was a circumspect man who never showed emotion. One morning, near dawn, he showed up in Michael's hospital room to check on him. He had just come from an eight-hour operation and his patient had died. He was so overcome with sadness that he cried. It was a rare display of humanity from this doctor or any doctor, and Michael never forgot it—or how the doctor made time to see him even though he was drained and exhausted.

* Michael went to see a specialist about his high incidence of kidney stones. The doctor was aware of the relationship between the stones and Crohn's, but was unaware of a remedy and determined to find one. The doctor then spent months at the Yale Medical School library researching the subject and ultimately came up with a drug called cholestyramine, which helped Michael for years.

* Michael's current gastroenterologist is a marathon runner and a man of boundless energy and good cheer. He's extremely accessible and returns calls even in the evening. He's also one of the only doctors we've encountered who actually turns to me, makes eye contact, and asks, "And how are you doing, Jane?"

The challenge for caregivers is how to communicate effectively with doctors who don't have much of a bedside manner, who can't get off the phone with you fast enough, who are gifted intellectually but don't have the personality to match. How do we force them to answer our questions without kidnapping them, tying them to a chair, and denying them food and water? Yes, they're busy, but part of the job of being a caregiver is to ask them what they're doing with our loved ones and why.

So, first come the questions; they should be written down beforehand so we don't waste everybody's time. In most instances, we're under stress, too overwhelmed to think clearly. Having the questions at our fingertips is definitely the way to go. Do you keep a pad and pen handy? Or make notes on your smart phone? Either way, some general topics to cover with any doctor:

* Please explain the diagnosis and prognosis.

* If there is no diagnosis, what tests do you plan to do to find one?

* Is there a specialist we need to consult?

* If there is a diagnosis, what is your treatment plan?

* How many of these cases have you treated/operated on before?

* Will the drugs have side effects and, if so, what are they?

* Will the patient be on a special diet?

* How long will the patient be in the hospital?

* If there is pain, how will it be managed?

* What are possible complications?

* Will you be overseeing the care personally?

* What's the best way to reach you?

Kelli Jackson, an RN in the Critical Care Unit at Cottage Hospital in Santa Barbara, agreed about writing down questions ahead of time—but she cautioned that we should pick our shots.

"When the doctor comes in, family members should say, 'I have four questions for you,'" she suggested. "It makes a doctor more accountable. Sometimes it's nice to get as many questions as possible answered by the nurse so there aren't as many for the physician, who doesn't want to stay long."

Why don't physicians want to stay long?

"They're busy," she said. "And they may not know all the answers, so they want to be in and out."

What's the best way to get them to stay then? Besides keeping the list of questions short?

"Family members should ask for a meeting," she said. "They should say, 'I know this isn't a good time. Can we set up a better time to sit down and talk about what's going to happen next?' Our physicians are up for that a hundred percent. They'll plan a time that's convenient for them."

Michael Lindenmayer, founding partner and chairman of the Caregiver Relief Fund, had a different take on doctors who don't return calls or answer questions to our satisfaction.

"Fire him," said Michael. "If that doctor is too busy to service you, look for another doctor. It's easy to say, 'Well, he's the only one in my insurance plan.' Sorry. You're not doing your homework. And if you're in an area where there's absolutely no health coverage and you have no ability to get anything done, then you have to take a serious look at your situation and ask, 'Am I in the right place?'"

Good advice, but I came up with my own way of compelling the doctor to stay in the room long enough to answer my questions.

Let me set the scene:

Michael was in a hospital in Florida recovering from surgery. Every day his surgeon would stop in for a quick look—and I do mean quick. I would be sitting in the chair by the bed and no sooner did I stand to approach the doctor than he was out the door, as if he had an allergy to caregivers. His behavior was worse than frustrating; it was crazy making.

"Doctor, do you have a second?" I'd ask.

"I'll be back tomorrow," he'd say and flee.

The next morning: "Doctor, I wanted to ask you about Michael's—"

"Oops. I'm late. Gotta go."

The next morning: "Doctor, how long do you think Michael will have to—"

"Let's see how he does today. Bye."

Okay, I thought. This is unacceptable.

The next morning I did not sit in my chair by the bed. I stood in the hall, outside Michael's room, and waited for the doctor to appear for his hit-and-run. The second he was inside the room, I moved in behind him, planting my feet in the threshold, blocking the door. In other words, he would have had to barrel me over to get out. Trapped!

I highly recommend this strategy to all caregivers who have found themselves in the same situation: just box the damn doctor in.

At the other end of the communication spectrum, Michael had a surgeon who couldn't stop talking—just not about anything related to Michael's health. He was a baseball fan and when he heard I'd written a book about the Yankees, he only wanted to talk about that. At first I was annoyed, but I realized that establishing a rapport with a doctor—about *anything*—is better than having no rapport at all.

When discussing the Doctor Issue with other caregivers, I discovered that quite a few have been frustrated by the lack of communication or the quality of the communication between them and their loved one's physician(s). Some anecdotes from our roundtable:

➤ **Yudi Bennett,** on the doctors who were treating her husband for lymphoma: "They kept telling us about the eighty-percent chance with the chemo and the fifty-percent chance with the bone marrow transplant. Nobody ever explained to us that Bob could die at the drop of a pin. My experience with cancer was that people declined gradually. I thought there would be time. Bob and I went to a wedding and the next day he was in the hospital with an infection and two days later he died. Those last two days of his life were the worst two days of mine. I was shell-shocked. So was Bob. I wish that somewhere in the journey the doctors had said to us, 'This could take a turn very suddenly.' Maybe if we'd gone into a support group, it would have come up. I don't know. But I fault doctors on this for always giving us the positive spin. It would have helped me to be a better caregiver to have had more information."

➤ **Jennifer DuBois,** on the palliative-care doctor who was overseeing her mother's treatment in the hospital: "My mother was supposed to be getting pain medicine so she would be kept comfortable. That's why we were there—to get her comfortable and into the hospice wing—but it just didn't go well at all because the medicine wasn't working anymore. We got very frustrated with the fact that nobody seemed to be taking charge of the situation. That's when I demanded that the doctor come down and look at her. I took him in the hall and got in his face. I said, 'My mother's situation is unacceptable and you need to do more.' He said, 'The only option that I have is to put her under anesthesia. You'll have to say your goodbyes.' It was really the only decision, and we made it as a family. But my advice is to demand to see the doctor and be straight with him. Nothing against nurses, but if they're just following doctors' orders, which is what they were doing in our case, and the doctors' orders aren't getting it done, then you need to demand to see the doctor. You have to be the squeaky wheel."

➤ **John Goodman,** on the doctors who were treating his wife for Cushing's syndrome at a New York hospital: "I was stunned how useless they were, shocked by the lack of care. My wife had a rare, serious case of Cushing's and the head of the endocrinology team was this woman who treated it like it was a toothache. I remember standing in the hall and reaming her out. Then she left on a planned vacation and we got another doctor. I shook the guy's hand and never saw him again—and I got a huge bill. I wrote him a letter saying, 'You are a crook. I was in that hospital from morning till night and I never saw you again. When were you treating my wife? Why are you billing her?' Finally, another doctor got involved and I remember sitting in the hallway with her saying, 'I need to deal with an endocrinologist who cares and can give me answers.' She said, 'Mr. Goodman, I promise I'll give you answers.' Thank God she did. She really walked the walk."

➤ **Suzanne Preisler,** on the surgeon who operated on her sister to determine whether her ovarian tumor was malignant: "The doctor was excellent, but his bedside manner was just terrible. He didn't even bother to tell us she had cancer. He walked into the waiting room after surgery, said she was okay, and walked out. I had been there waiting with my husband, Jerome, for eight hours. Maybe the surgeon had spoken to my sister's husband somewhere else, but I guess he didn't feel he had to talk to her sister. So Jerome blocked his way into the elevator and he started answering our questions. Until that point, he was just going to leave us there."

➤ **Karen Prince,** on the neurologist in the hospital who treated her forty-nine-year-old husband immediately after he suffered the stroke: "He upset me very much. He said to me, in front of Andy, over his bed, 'The only thing he has going for him is his age.' I said, 'Excuse me, doctor? Could we talk in the hallway?' You'd think he would have had the smarts about that because we didn't know what Andy took in and what he didn't. I had no use for that doctor after that."

➤ **Toni Sherman,** on the orthopedist who treated her daughter Courtney's severely infected foot after prior surgery at another clinic had failed to catch the infection: "I started talking to this orthopedist about lawsuits. He got really upset. He said, 'I am not going to testify. I am not going to be involved in this. I think you are absolutely wrong to pursue this.' My initial reaction was: Oh my God, what have I done? I realized I allowed his reaction to make me retreat, as if I'd been a bad girl, and how easy it is for them to do it and how accepting I am of their ire. I think he could have handled it in a very different way. He was a doctor and I was the mother of his patient and I was terrified of what the eventuality of all this might be, which was that my daughter could lose her foot. But he was a very good orthopedist. So I just stopped my rant completely and we went on. It left me feeling that doctor-patient relationships are complicated. I think when doctors are approached about the misbehavior of other doctors, they react with fear that they'll be drawn into it. But maybe it was simply that he thought I was a nasty little shrew."

My goal is not to beat up on doctors in this chapter. But Toni is right; doctor-patient relationships *are* complicated and doctor-caregiver relationships can be downright rocky. Personally, I worry way too much about being chatty and entertaining when I'm around doctors so that they'll like me (and presumably be nice to Michael). It's pretty pathetic. Why are they so intimidating?

"They almost have to be," psychotherapist Tina B. Tessina told me. "You can't go cutting into people and making life and death decisions with your heart bleeding all the time. You'd never survive. So in order to be good doctors, they have to pull away."

Michael Lindenmayer thinks that part of the reason doctors are hard to deal with is that they're under tremendous stress themselves.

"They want to help," he said, "but they are getting annihilated by the medical system right now. Their payments are going down and their patient load is going up. So when you're going to them, you have to know what to expect from them. And they're not miracle workers; families have to really get with the program of being their own advocate and their own coordinator."

The good news is that many, many doctors don't pull away, do spend time with you, do make you feel cared for and attended to. Judy Hartnett, for example, has found all of the above in the doctor who treats her husband, Paul, for MS: "Our internist now is as bright as anybody I've ever met and equally kind. He said from the get go, 'I will take care of both of you. You don't ever have to sit in an ER alone, Judy. Here's my cell.' That was my goal—to find somebody that was on my team."

We all need to find doctors like Judy's. In the meantime, it's huge just knowing they're out there.

CHAPTER 5

How to Turn Even the Crankiest Nurses/ Aides/Medical Personnel into Buddies

- - - - - - - - - - - - - -

"You thank the nurses all the time, for every little thing they do and every big thing they do. And then you thank them again."

—JENNIFER DUBOIS, caregiver

Tell me if this has happened to you: You're taking your loved one to the doctor. Or maybe you're visiting him/her at the hospital or assisted-living facility. You're exhausted, anxious, so vulnerable that a cross look from a stranger in the elevator is enough to bring you to your knees. You arrive and what do you find? A receptionist, nurse, or nurse's aide with a full-on *attitude*.

For example, during one of Michael's hospitalizations that was particularly worrisome, I was about as strung out as I'd ever been—anxious about his health, missing him at home, desperately needing a good night's sleep. I yearned for a nurturing presence at the hospital, a compassionate member of his medical team who would—I don't know—say something soothing, hug me, be the human equivalent of a bowl of Cream of Wheat.

Instead, what I got was a nurse whom the rest of the staff had nicknamed Big Linda in order to differentiate her from another nurse named Linda, who was petite. Big Linda was about six feet three and 250 pounds and somewhere in her forties. She wore a scowl that could scare small animals. She was brusque with everyone, and several nurses had transferred out of the unit so as not to have to deal with her. She was an equal opportunity grouch, in other words.

What made Big Linda stand out (in addition to her size) was that everyone else at the hospital was so kind and attentive—from the charge nurse right down to the woman who scrubbed the floor.

Michael tried to befriend Big Linda to the extent that he smiled at her a lot and hoped she'd smile back.

"Didn't work," he said about his efforts. "She's just an unhappy person. Nobody around here likes her."

"Is she giving you good care?" I asked.

"Good enough," he said.

That wasn't good enough for me. I was determined to charm Big Linda, being the pleaser that I am—someone who operates under the notion that everybody should be nice to everybody so we can all live in one happy Kumbaya world.

I tried being nice to Big Linda.

"How are you today, Linda?" I asked when she stormed into Michael's room to flush his IV line. She had heavy feet to go with her heavy body, so you could always hear her coming.

"Fn." (I think she said "Fine," but she mumbled it so I couldn't exactly tell.)

"You're amazing the way you come in to check on Michael so often. We really appreciate it."

Silence.

"Must be a long shift," I nattered on. "Isn't it, like, seven to seven?"

She grunted and turned to go.

"Do you like cake?" I said in a burst of spontaneity.

She rolled her eyes. "Why?"

"Just wondering," I said, remembering that my friend Laurie bakes over 300 little loaf-size chocolate cakes every Christmas, wraps them in Saran wrap with a bow on top, and gives them out to doctors, nurses, and receptionists, not to mention manicurists, bikini waxers, and every other person who performs a service for her. They go over really well, even with the most hard-to-crack sourpusses, and for that alone Laurie should win the Nobel Peace Prize.

I left the hospital that night, stopped at the supermarket, bought a box of Duncan Hines chocolate cake mix and baked a loaf, and then wrapped it the same way Laurie wraps hers. (No, my cake wasn't from scratch, but I figured it was the thought that counted.)

The next morning I presented it to Big Linda when she came into Michael's room to bark that it was time for his medication.

"For you," I said with outstretched arms, holding the cake tenderly, as if it were a newborn baby.

"What's that?" she said with her perpetual scowl. You would have thought I'd just handed her a pile of manure.

"A chocolate cake," I said. "To thank you for taking such good care of my husband. Maybe you can have a piece on your lunch break today."

Big Linda looked stunned. Her large frame stood motionless for several awkward seconds before she reached out for the cake and smelled it. "Doesn't have nuts in it, does it?"

That was her response—to ask me if the cake had nuts in it. "Nope. No nuts."

"Okay then."

And off she went with the cake.

I turned to Michael. "So much for that," I said. "Big Linda couldn't even acknowledge an act of kindness."

We speculated about her home life and wondered why she was so sullen, and then just when we were really getting into our analysis of her emotional psyche, back she came—this time lugging a huge chair. It was like a Barcalounger only without the reclining part and she had trouble squeezing it through the door. She set it down in front of Michael's bed and then motioned for me to get up from the visitor's chair (the same model that was in every patient's room) and wedged the Barcalounger into the corner in its place.

"There," she said, wiping the sweat off her gigantic forehead. "Use that from now on. It'll be more comfortable."

"Oh. Wow. Thank you very—"

Before I could finish the sentence, she was gone.

I leaned back in my new chair and grinned. I felt like a queen on a throne. Big Linda was human after all.

Should every caregiver bake a chocolate cake for every cantankerous medical person? Ilene Brenner, the ER doc I interviewed, said that food went over well with her and her colleagues. Heidi Holly, executive director at the Friendship Center, an adult day care center in Santa Barbara, agreed that food is always welcome, but she had another suggestion for caregivers.

"Write a letter to the editor of the local newspaper," she said. "Publicize us. Let the community know how grateful you are that you found this jewel that helps your mom or dad. Or just come up to our staff and say, 'Thank you for what you do to help my mom or dad live with dignity and joy.'"

Since most of my experiences have involved nurses, I was curious about what they think of caregivers. What are the ways we get on their nerves, what are the ways we endear ourselves to them, and how can we be the best advocates for our loved ones? Kelli Jackson, RN in the Critical Care Unit at Santa Barbara Cottage Hospital, was kind enough to let me ask her everything I ever wanted to know on the subject.

Jane: *Do you like the family members of your patients or are we a huge pain?*

Kelli: The family members become our patients in a way. They're the ones we're talking to, the ones we're reassuring, and the ones we're updating on the patient's condition.

Jane: *It's scary to have a loved one in the Critical Care Unit. Do most family members behave calmly or are they on the hysterical side?*

Kelli: It totally depends on why the patient was admitted. You've got the family members who've been there with their chronically ill loved one five or six times. They're a little bit calmer because they understand the system. But if you have a twenty-year-old guy with a walnut allergy who can't speak and can't breathe and is on a ventilator and he was completely well that same morning, the family is going to react much differently. What matters most is how information is given to them when they get there. Sometimes it's delivered by residents, who may or may not know what they're talking about. Sometimes it's delivered by an attending physician, who may be very involved with that family and knows the case inside and out. Sometimes it's delivered by nursing because we're at the bedside. But the nursing coat is very different than the white coat.

Jane: *Speaking of which, nurses don't wear uniforms anymore—at least not that I've seen. It's almost impossible to tell who's a nurse, who's an aide, who's a tech. What's up with that?*

Kelli: I've worked at places where we've had to wear uniforms—like all the nurses wore blue and the techs wore a different color. The research definitely is out there in terms of patient dissatisfaction— that it's a problem when they don't know who's who.

Jane: *Once caregivers figure out who the nurse is, can you suggest a diplomatic way for us to speak up if we think he or she is doing some- thing wrong? Nobody wants to go off on anybody, but sometimes nerves get frayed.*

Kelli: If a family member is mad about something that's not my fault, I'll listen and try to hear why they're angry and help them see the light.

Jane: *What if it* is *your fault?*

Kelli: We all make mistakes. We all say we're coming back with that blanket and we forget. Years ago a guy asked me for two Tums and I totally forgot. I went back a few hours later and he said, "Were you making those from scratch?" It was so perfect because he was being funny instead of angry. We had built a trust. I had done what I said I was going to do every time except that time, so it was okay. We are wrong sometimes and the families are rightfully angry.

Jane: *So what should we do about that anger?*

Kelli: There's a chain of command. If you're not getting what you want from the nurse, you can talk to the charge nurse, who oversees the floor for that day. If that doesn't work, you can talk to the nurse manager, who manages our floor. And then there's the nursing supervisor, who manages the hospital on that particular day.

Jane: *Don't you get pissed off if somebody goes over your head?*

Kelli: No, but I wish they'd tell me the problem first. One thing that's frustrating is when a patient has a problem with something we do and they tell the family member but not us. So the angry family member calls and says, "My father is cold. He needs a blanket." Or "He's hungry." I say, "Well, the patient hasn't asked for anything to eat. I can't read minds." The patient needs to state his or her needs, and if they're not met then it's justifiable for a family member to come and ask why.

Jane: *Do more people get angry today than in the past? I think there's a lot of pent-up frustration with the health-care system in general.*

Kelli: Definitely. People don't have as much health-care coverage. They're sicker by the time they come into the hospital, so the family members are more stressed.

Plus, there's the economy. Maybe the family member has just lost a job. It goes back to our culture. People don't talk about their feelings so it all kind of builds up, and then a nurse in a hospital says, "I'll be back," and doesn't come back right away, and people snap.

Jane: *Do you ever snap? You're in a high-stress job, after all.*

Kelli: I'm like everybody else. If I'm having a bad day, I'm a little shorter, a little less accommodating.

Jane: *What constitutes "having a bad day" when it comes to dealing with family members? Are there specific things we do that drive you nuts?*

Kelli: It's the worst when they say, "Can we have butter for my father?" And you go to the kitchen and you get the butter and then you come back and they say, "Can you get him cranberry juice too?" I go, "Really? I was just in the kitchen where the butter came from." So here's a tip for caregivers: If you're going to ask a nurse for a variety of things, ask for them all at once so she doesn't have to make several trips and build up resentment toward you. And then there are the caregivers who ask for things for themselves. Like: "Can you get me coffee?" That bugs me. I want to say, "Get your own coffee in the cafeteria. You can leave the patient alone for five minutes."

Jane: *Do you commiserate with other nurses about us caregivers? Make jokes about us? Come on. Be honest.*

Kelli: We do. Some of the wives are a little much.

Jane: *The wives? Uh-oh. Why?*

Kelli: They'll feed their husband, who's perfectly capable of feeding himself. Or I'll be talking to their husband, and they'll answer every question. The women definitely want to control the situation. I see them stand there while their husband is having a bowel movement. I'll say, "You could go out of the room and give him some privacy."

Jane: *Yikes. I've never done that!*

Kelli: Maybe it's their way of feeling useful. But the husband doesn't always want them there. He may want a break. That's something for caregivers to really understand—that the patient sometimes needs to be left alone.

I don't know how many times patients have whispered to me, "Can you please just tell them to leave for awhile? Make them go to dinner?" It's really important for families to give the patients some rest and quiet.

Jane: *They tell you they want us to leave?*

Kelli: Definitely. Obviously, it's important to have people call and come and visit, but it's also important for the patients to have quiet time. So, my tip for caregivers is this: have one contact person that will talk, text, tweet, e-mail about the patient's condition so he doesn't have to tell everyone the same thing over and over again.

Jane: *What's the best way for caregivers to show their appreciation for all you do? I once baked a cake for a nurse.*

Kelli: Writing a letter is great because letters are always very genuine. Sometimes people just want to say goodbye and thank you. Or sometimes they say they appreciate it if you had a meaningful conversation with them. It can be a very intimate time when you talk to a nurse while your loved one is in the hospital sick or, in some cases, dying. Nurses are safe, so family members will talk about all kinds of things with you.

Jane: *Is it harder for you when the patient is dying?*

Kelli: No. I love the death-and-dying moments because I feel I can bring so much to them. The horrible transition is going to happen no matter what, so I try to anticipate what the family members need. I listen. I'm compassionate. I cry with them. I hug them. I just took care of a dying patient whose daughter was my age. She wanted to know what was going to happen with her father, so we talked about that. Then we talked about life and what it was like being our age, not married, and no kids. When she was leaving, she gave me a hug and said, "Thanks so much. I needed that conversation." We were truthful with each other, not superficial. And, believe it or not, the end-of-life moments can be fun. The family members tell funny stories about their loved one. I'll say, "What was your favorite thing about your husband?" Or "Where did you guys meet?" I've had some really good moments with my family members.

Jane: *That's pretty amazing, Kelli. Is there anything else you think caregivers should know?*

Kelli: Yes. Touch the patient. Touch is huge. Sometimes family members just stand at the door or sit in the chair reading the newspaper. Don't forget to touch your loved one.

Jane: *I won't.*

CHAPTER 6

When Loved Ones Take on a Different Personality and You Start Wishing They'd Disappear

- - - - - - - - - - - - - -

"Dark thoughts are perfectly natural. They don't necessarily mean you want the person to leave the premises. It's the disease you want to go away. You have to separate out the person from the disease."
—SUZANNE MINTZ, cofounder of the National Family Caregivers Association

I don't remember much about my father, since I was so young when he died of brain cancer. By all accounts, he was a loving and generous man—someone who laughed and liked to dance and enjoyed a close relationship with his family. I do remember that on those rare occasions when he was well enough to get dressed and go to his office, he would come home with a pint of Breyer's vanilla ice cream just for me. We had a window seat in our living room with a view onto the street. At five o'clock sharp, I'd hop into that seat and wait like a frisky puppy for his car to drive up and for him to walk through our front door and call out, "I brought you something, Janie!"

He was such a nice man that it was inconceivable that he would nearly kill me.

Okay, I'm being totally melodramatic here. He didn't nearly kill me and this isn't one of *those* stories—not even close; it just felt as if he had turned scary.

What happened was this: I was about three or four and I was sitting on the floor. My father, a tall man, was walking toward me, theoretically to crouch down to play with me. Instead, he had a seizure, lost his balance, and fell into a spastic heap across my body. I have no memory of the violent impact, only a hazy recall of having had the wind knocked out of me and of everybody clamoring to get me to the hospital.

I was fine; nothing was bruised or broken. There was just the residue of fear I felt around my father from then on. Inside my little-girl head, he went from nice to creepy in one terrible moment, and, although I tried not to show it, I became uncomfortable around him.

Two or three years later, when he was so ill that he was bedridden and near death, I made a bizarre game out of him, a freak show. I played carnival barker and invited kids over to stand in his doorway and take a sneak peek at the bald, blind, paralyzed man under the covers—the man who didn't bat an eyelash, let alone mow the lawn, walk the dog, or wash the car like other fathers in the neighborhood. "Step right up and get a look at my dying daddy!" was how I'd lure them in. Since I was the only kid in my class with a parent on the verge of the Big D, I figured I'd use it to my advantage and boost my Q-rating at school. I didn't sell tickets, but only because the idea didn't occur to me.

I'm ashamed to admit all this—I still can't believe I actually marketed my own father; I guess I was exhibiting the PR skills that would lead to my career as a book publicist later in life—but our thoughts are our thoughts. I was very young and I didn't understand the first thing about death or illness, since no one seemed inclined to explain it to me. All I knew was that I used to have a father who brought me ice cream and then I had a father who stared into space, drooling.

I only wish my adult self could make him materialize so I could apologize to him, tell him that I just didn't get it, and say, "I realize now that the horror-movie guy wasn't you, Dad; it was the cancer."

Illness can change the personality and/or social skills of our loved ones, often radically, and as caregivers we have to find ways of dealing with these changes. The problem is particularly acute when the loved one is suffering from Alzheimer's or dementia.

Michael has been my ultimate Jekyll and Hyde, and the stunning turnabouts in his personality nearly derailed our marriage several times. When I met him, he was gentle, laid-back, respectful, not to mention my type physically (lean but broad-shouldered, muscular but not muscle-bound, handsome but not pretty).

Then came his Crohn's flare-ups, which usually necessitated high doses of steroids. Suddenly, he wasn't handsome; he was bloated and moonfaced. Suddenly, he wasn't gentle; he was irascible. Suddenly, he wasn't the man I married, and I vacillated between praying he wouldn't die and wishing he would.

Yes, I wished he would die. Whenever he'd fly into a prednisone-fueled fury, I would fantasize about all the ways I could kill him—from smothering him with a pillow to "fixing" the brakes in his car (like I'd ever know how to do that; I can't even pump my own gas). I didn't really want him to die, obviously. What I wanted to die was the Crohn's.

One incident in particular stands out:

We were preparing to move from Florida to California—a stressful time for anyone, even without the complication of an illness. I had done the bulk of the packing for us, labeling the cartons, lining them up, organizing the whole affair. Michael was not only taking prednisone at the time but testosterone. Throw in his nightly cocktail of Mount Gay Rum and tonic, and he was a walking nightmare, prone to angry outbursts that would seemingly come from nowhere.

"The kitchen stuff goes in this pile," I said, pointing to boxes full of pots and pans. We had just finished dinner and were standing in the hallway between the kitchen and dining room.

"Who put you in charge?" Michael said accusingly, his voice raised, his complexion flushed. "What if I want to put my boxes here instead?"

I was taken aback. "What boxes?"

"Whatever boxes I want!"

Huh?

"Okay, what's really going on?" I asked. "Are you upset about something?"

"It's your fault that we're even moving."

"My fault that we're—" I stopped and stared at him. We had decided—together—that after seven years in Florida we were up for a change of scenery. Both of us had wanted to see what living in California would be like. Both of us wanted the Left Coast experience. Both of us thought the time was right to sell our house and embark on an adventure. I certainly hadn't put a gun to his head.

"This was all your idea and it sucks. I'm not going!"

I launched into a defense of myself and then explained that we'd already hired the moving company, rented a new place, and booked a flight, and that if he didn't want to move he should have mentioned it a tad earlier in the proceedings.

Big mistake. You can't reason with someone who's incapable of reason. If only I'd known that then.

At one point during my speech, Michael exploded. I mean really lost it. His eyes bugged out of his head and his cheeks kind of inflated like a cartoon character and he punched the wall several times. (I'm so bourgeois that I actually said to myself, "But we just had it painted.") He cursed at me and carried on like a child having a tantrum and it was all so bizarre that I could only step back and observe the insanity. I hated my husband, the whack job, and I wanted my husband, the sweetheart, back.

When I mentioned the incident to Michael the other day, as I was writing it up for this book, he said, "I remember feeling completely out of control and there was no stopping it. That's what 'roid rage' is all about—being out of control."

I get that now. I got it an hour after the incident. Once I had a good cry and calmed down a little, I realized that, as a caregiver, I not only had to make the distinction between Michael and the chemicals that were distorting his personality, but I also had a responsibility to discuss his drugs with his doctor.

The result? We eliminated two of the three troublemakers: the testosterone and the Mount Gay Rum. Life with Michael improved, and we were off to California feeling more hopeful about the future and each other. But his behavior under the influence really rattled me and I don't think I could have stayed in the marriage if he'd continued to be a monster.

Suzanne Mintz summed up my situation and that of many other caregivers this way: "When it gets to the level of abuse," she said, "you've got a decision to make. It's just like if a wife is beaten: Are you going to put up with this? *Can* you put up with this? You are allowed to say no."

Good point. We are allowed to say no.

I asked the members of my newly formed support group if they'd ever been plagued by dark thoughts—from the secret desire to bump off a loved one (or themselves) to the urge to just walk away.

➤ **Barbara Blank,** while her ninety-six-year-old father was still living with her before moving into a seniors' community: "My father's rages are more extreme now because there's clearly some dementia there. Like yesterday he insisted on doing something in his apartment. We went over and I did it his way and it didn't work. He started screaming obscenities at me, and I got really angry back for the first time. I said, 'How dare you talk to me like that! Call one of your other wonderful children and tell them to do this.'

"He calmed down, but I don't like losing it. I thought, I'm gonna kill myself. And then I thought, No, wait a minute. I'm gonna kill him! He just isn't the same person anymore. Sometimes I look at him when he gets nasty and I divorce myself from the fact that he's my father and say, 'He's just a person.' I have a box in my brain. If something's really bad, I put it in the box and seal it up. I've learned how to do that."

➤ **Harriet Brown,** during the time she was overseeing the family-based treatment plan for her anorexic daughter, cooking for her, sitting with her and making sure she ate every meal every day: "I guess the closest I came to getting in the car and driving away were those one or two nights when I threw a lot of dishes around the kitchen. But then I'd just think, 'Well, you have no choice. You have to keep going.'"

➤ **Linda Dano,** on her father's behavior before she realized he had Alzheimer's: "Right after my father came to live with us, his behavior was so crazy he ended up in the psych ward. It was literally like the movie *Snake Pit* where people would run by you and go, '*Whoooooo!*' And when he stopped eating, I gave him the feeding tube, not knowing what was wrong with him. Once he was in the nursing home, he would cry all day long. I went through a period where I was going to kill him myself—put something in his feeding tube and let him peacefully go to heaven. I was so guilty. I should have taken him out of there, hired three nurses, and given him morphine for a week. I never forgave myself that I couldn't help him. To this day I haven't forgiven myself."

➤ **John Goodman,** when his wife was in the ICU after surgery for her Cushing's syndrome: "She was in a room for a week with no windows, so there was no day or night, no sense of time. She was raving crazy. They called it 'ICU psychosis.' She would bite me, bite the nurses, even try to bite the doctors. For a brief while they literally tied her to the bed. There were days when I'd walk in the door and she'd smile and know who I was, and there were other days when I'd walk in and it would be awful.

"One time I walked in with a bacon-and-egg sandwich and she threw it on the floor. It was eight o'clock in the morning—not the way I wanted to start my day. It was very difficult. But whenever I'd go in the hall and break down, my daughters would say, 'You know that's not Mom. You know she's crazy right now. But this is treatable and she's going to get better.' They were there and they helped me get through it."

➤ **Judy Harnett,** when her husband was hospitalized and treated with prednisone: "The last time was a nightmare. They just pumped him up with steroids. He was bug-eyed and insane. He didn't even know who I was a couple of times, and he was mean and nasty. At least it was while he was in the hospital so I didn't have to deal with it by myself. I never wanted him to hurry up and die, except when he was on the steroids."

➤ **Cecilia Johnston,** on her mother's descent into Alzheimer's and her own reaction to it: "My mom's memory is like Swiss cheese and you just never know which hole you're going to drop into. I'm at the point now where I want her to die. I love her more than anything in the whole wide world, but her father had dementia and her great-aunt did and my mom was their caregiver. She said, 'I never ever want to be in this position. Please kill me if I am.' I said, 'Mom, that's all well and good, but I'd get thrown in prison. If that's what you want, you need to do that.' Unfortunately, she didn't commit suicide when she had the capability."

➤ **Harold Schwartz,** on caring for both his son with ALS and his wife with Parkinson's: "When we would go to DC to take care of our son, I would literally shower him and brush his teeth and clean him up after the toilet, and I would think to myself, we're back to him being a baby because I did this for him when he was six months old. It came pretty naturally, but sure I got depressed. There were times when I'd say, 'I wish this was all over.' Did I ever say, 'Why me?' No. A lot of people ask, 'Why me?' My answer is 'Why *not* me?' I could pick up the newspaper every day and read about people who have so much worse problems than I do—people who face devastation all over the world. To me life is a giant crapshoot. Things happen. You're lucky or you're not lucky. You don't have the luxury of saying, 'I'm not going to do this'—not when you're talking about the people you love."

➤ **Toni Sherman,** after her ninety-four-year-old mother fell and sustained brain damage prior to her diagnosis of cancer: "While she was in the hospital she had trouble recognizing her husband and was unclear about a lot of things. She was also argumentative and had never been before. When she got home, I went out to pick up some prescriptions for her. I got back and her husband said to me, 'Your mother thinks that you and I are having an affair.' I was stunned. I turned to my mother and said, 'Why would you think that of me?'

"She was my mother and she was accusing me of the worst kind of betrayal. I had to leave. I was devastated. When she was diagnosed with cancer, she came home with hospice and was pleasant, pliable, able to laugh. But she had been slipping so badly that her responses could be weird. It was like dealing with another person, and it was hideous to watch. I wanted her to go. I'd had it."

➤ **John Shore,** on the experience of caring for his eighty-five-year-old father despite not having seen him in years: "My father is a terrible, terrible person, but when you've got a parent who's gone down, you can't just write them off. You want to run away and say, 'Not my problem; I live all the way across the country.' But you know you'll go to your grave not feeling good about yourself. So my feeling was, I should go. And, as I expected, my dad was horrendous to me.

"I handled it by just functioning—cooking and cleaning and doing what I was doing. I never got upset. Well, there was one time when we were driving. He's always in a rush. I was taking him to the drug store and it was pouring rain with bad visibility, and he really wanted me to run a red light. I came to my naturally slow break at the light and he screamed with such tremendous volume and venom and moved to strike me—just raised his hand like he was going to pop me on the side of the head. I can't say that didn't bother me. But I didn't flinch.

"Everybody has a singular challenge in life—to figure out who they are in relation to their parents. You don't take care of that? Nothing else in your life ever works. Also, when you're taking care of your husband or your father or your mother, you're suffering for a greater good, for somebody else's well-being. It's an honor. So that's why I didn't mind being with my dad. I'd go back there again."

➤ **Diane Sylvester,** on driving back and forth from Santa Barbara to LA to care for her mother with dementia: "It was pure hell for a couple of years. My mother was living alone. We tried live-in people a couple of times, but she just went berserk. Then she started doing really bizarre things, like talking to her purse, thinking it was the telephone, forgetting how to turn the TV on and off, making bizarre calls at all times of the day and night, and not going to bed; she would sit in her chair and just stay there all night long. Every once in awhile during my numerous trips to LA, I'd just mentally crash on the freeway. I would call my husband and say, 'You need to come. I can't do this. I can't face what's happening down here.' And he would get in the car and come down."

To sum up, being a caregiver inevitably means experiencing one or more of the following emotions:

* Guilt.

* Helplessness.

* Frustration.

* Rage.

* Resentment.

* Sadness.

* Loss.

Good, good times, right?

But here's the thing. There *are* good times if you're open to them. The trick is to acknowledge your dark thoughts and feelings, resign yourself to getting fed up with the whole mess on occasion, and confide in people who won't look at you as if you're Casey Anthony. If you share the dark thoughts with somebody else—actually say them out loud to a friend, therapist, or the guy standing next to you on the subway—you'll feel better. You will.

CHAPTER 7

How to Wait Out Waiting Rooms

"Make sure you're up every twenty minutes—walking around the room or bending down to tie your shoes. Any kind of little movement is a very good thing. It resets your body and helps you relieve stress."
—NANCY KALISH, certified health coach

Michael had surgery twice in 2010 and both times I spent hours in the surgical waiting room, waiting—waiting for the doctor to emerge from the OR with news, waiting for a hospital volunteer to tell me I could go back into recovery to see my husband, waiting for him to wake up and prove to me he wasn't dead.

Waiting is not my strong suit, so this aspect of being a caregiver has been yet another adjustment for me.

Here's what I've learned about waiting rooms: they're not libraries. They're not even Barnes & Nobles. It's hard to concentrate on the book you've brought to read because the people on either side of you are talking and distracting you. You don't mean to eavesdrop on their conversations, but you can't help it. Sometimes you want to stand up and yell, "Could everybody please shut up," but you've been raised to behave better than that, besides which, security would probably come and cart you away.

I've brought my laptop to waiting rooms and tried to write. Can't do it.

I've tried browsing the Internet in search of news items with catchy headlines, but they're no help either.

What's the best way to kill time, in my experience? Either ask a friend or family member to sit with you while you wait and help take your mind off the fact that you're sick with worry, or bond with the other people in the waiting room who are just as sick with worry as you are.

I've done both, and they're equally effective time killers.

Michael's first surgery last year was a "resection," which means that a surgeon cuts away the inflamed portions of his intestines and reattaches the healthy ends. I brought along my friend Melodie to wait with me. She's a writer of mystery novels and short stories, so her imagination works overtime as mine does, and we spent a couple of hours cooking up a plot involving the family of six on the other side of the room—from names for their characters to which ones were murder suspects. I'm sure the people sitting next to us thought we were nuts, but they seemed riveted by every word.

Speaking of the people sitting next to us, they were so riveted that when Michael's surgeon entered the waiting room and sat down with us, they leaned in so they wouldn't miss his report.

"Michael's out of surgery," said the doctor. "It was more difficult than I expected, because he's had so many previous resections, but we cut away all the scar tissue and he should do fine."

"How long will he have to stay in the hospital?" I asked.

"About a week if all goes well," he said.

"What complications might there be?" I asked.

"There's always a risk of infection with abdominal surgery," said the doctor, "but we're minimizing that by letting the incision heal from the inside out."

"So no stitches or staples?" I said.

"Right," he said. "Only underneath—the dissolving ones."

"*You mean you left him open?*" asked the woman to my right, clearly upset.

"We often do that," said the doctor, turning to face her. "Much better chance of avoiding a bacterial infection."

"*But how will he heal if he's not sewn up?*" she asked, clapping her hand over her mouth in a show of dismay.

"We'll have a home health-care nurse who—" The doctor paused in mid-sentence and glanced back at me. "Do you know her?"

"I don't," I said.

"Not a friend?"

"No."

"Family member?"

"Nope."

We all laughed. Waiting rooms are not conducive to privacy, and while that particular incident was funny because Michael was, indeed, fine, it seems to me that hospitals should designate an area in which doctors and family members can speak in confidence, without interlopers, as well-meaning as they may be. I know there are conference areas, and doctors often use them when the postsurgical news is dire. But how about using them for run-of-the-mill conversations too?

For Michael's second surgery (he was not fine, it turned out—more on that later), I went solo for my long stint in the waiting room and struck up a conversation with a woman whose husband was also going under the knife. We bonded initially over our shared concern for our spouses but quickly moved on to our favorite local restaurants, the movies we'd seen, the state of the economy, our bewilderment over the public's fascination with the Kardashian sisters, you name it. We never exchanged names and phone numbers or vowed to stay in touch; there was an implicit understanding that our friendship was based strictly on our mutual need to kill time. And it did kill time. Michael was out of surgery before I knew it.

So by all means bring a book or a laptop or an iPad if you have the ability to tune out all the noise. But my suggestion is to either bring a friend or make a new one.

One of the things I did not do while I waited in waiting rooms was get my butt up off the chair. Not to use the restroom. Not to visit the cafeteria. Not to pace in the hall. And certainly not to actually take a walk around the block. God forbid I should leave the room just at the moment that the doctor came looking for me or Michael woke up and asked for me.

And so I sat for hours, knowing it was as unhealthy as eating a dozen Krispy Kremes. I'm a writer and my lifestyle is nothing if not sedentary; people have been telling me for years that sitting is bad for your heart, bad for your circulation, bad for just about everything.

What I didn't get is that by moving around even the slightest bit, I could have been relieving stress in that waiting room. That's the takeaway from Nancy Kalish, a board-certified health coach who counsels both individuals and corporate clients and writes about health issues for national magazines.

"What's happening when caregivers are under stress is that their bodies are pumping out an enormous amount of the stress hormones adrenaline and cortisol, which can have a really debilitating effect," she explained. "New research shows that sitting for long periods of time is related to increased death rates and that just getting up and walking around makes a big difference. So if you can go out and walk around the block, do it."

Enough said. The next time I'm in the waiting room, I won't wait to get up and move. I seriously don't want my death rate to increase; plus I wouldn't mind reducing the cottage cheese on my thighs.

CHAPTER 8

The Hospital Room Etiquette Miss Manners Never Told Us About

"When I go out to the lobby and introduce myself to family members, I say, 'Here are the rules. You can come every day except for seven to eight thirty in the morning, and you can have two people at the bedside.' I lay that right out."

—KELLI JACKSON, RN, Santa Barbara Cottage Hospital

Depending on your loved one's health insurance policy, he/she will either be entitled to a private room in a hospital or nursing facility or be stuck with a roommate.

Michael has had some lovely roomies who were quiet, obeyed the rules, and eased the boredom with occasional chitchat. But as his caregiver, I've been more concerned with the roommates who were less than desirable and required intervention.

His first crazy roommate actually provided us with comic relief, so I didn't take any action against him—initially. He was a guy who'd been stabbed in the abdomen at a party; his girlfriend, he told us, had been in a jealous rage and couldn't control herself.

She had good reason to be jealous, as it turned out. I came to visit Michael one night and the curtain was drawn between the two beds.

"He's getting a blow job," Michael whispered, nodding at his roommate.

"*What?*"

"Listen."

Sure enough, there was a woman in there with Mr. Stud, and his moaning and groaning and "Oh, yeah, baby" were unmistakable signs that they were doing more than discussing the weather. When she was finished, he told her he loved her and she told him she loved him and off she went. Five minutes later he was on the phone with another woman.

"Hey, baby," we heard him say. "You coming to see me tonight?"

Michael and I looked at each other and burst into hysterics.

This guy had a parade of ladies who'd show up to service him—one right after the other—and he was a master at scheduling their visits so they'd think they were his one and only. Talk about an operator. Yes, we were grossed out by his behavior after awhile, but I never felt it was my place to report it—until one of the nocturnal visits overlapped with another and a catfight ensued.

Michael was trying to rest and the screeching was too much. I stepped outside and asked a nurse to quell the disturbance. The next day the horn-dog patient was discharged, and that was the end of that.

One of my pet peeves when it comes to roommates are those with family members who ignore the "only two at a time" rule. I walked into Michael's room one afternoon and there were ten people gathered around the patient in the next bed. And of course, they'd confiscated my chair and pulled it over to their side of the room. They'd brought food, which reeked of garlic, and were on their cell phones constantly and one of them fancied herself as a spiritual guru and wouldn't stop talking about "negative auras." I couldn't get over this patient's family and their lack of consideration for *my* patient, who was too sick to tell them to shut up.

I went outside to the nurses' station. "Isn't there a rule about two visitors to a patient?" I asked the staff at large, since I couldn't find Michael's nurse.

"What's the problem?" said one of them with wild disinterest, a blonde who was much too busy braiding her hair to make eye contact.

"There's a convention going on in 314," I said, referring to Michael's room number. "My husband needs to rest."

"Ask them to leave," said the blonde.

I stepped closer to the desk. "No, *you* ask them to leave. It's your job."

I'm very easygoing except when I'm not. I've worked as a hospital volunteer for years and at two different hospitals. Rules are rules, and the nursing staff is supposed to enforce them for the good of their patients.

The blonde pouted but nevertheless did as I asked. The family filed out and the room was blessedly quiet. Bottom line? It may be the nurses' job to restore order, but as a caregiver it's our job to make them do it.

My role as the Roommate Police was never clearer than during Michael's most recent hospitalization. The roommate was a solitary sort—no visitors, no phone calls, no TV watching. That was the good news. One afternoon a doctor who appeared to be new to his case came to see him.

"Hello," said the doctor to the roommate. "I've been brought in to consult."

One of the facts of hospital life is that you overhear private conversations between patients and doctors whether you intend to or not. I'm very sensitive to HIPAA, the law that mandates patient confidentiality, but hospitals and other facilities—doctors' offices too—need to do a better job of making it practical. I mean have you ever been to your primary-care doc's office for an appointment? Of course you have, so you know the drill. You sit in the waiting room and suddenly it's your turn to go in and you realize it's your turn because a nurse or receptionist *screams out your name.* Some confidentiality, right?

Anyhow, here's what happened next between the doctor and Michael's roommate.

"So how long have you had TB?" asked the doctor.

I did a double take. Tuberculosis is one of the most contagious diseases around, and Michael, who has the immune system of a mayfly, had been sharing a toilet and sink with this roommate. The guy should have been in isolation.

I hopped up and went to blab to the first nurse I spotted.

"I hate to compromise a patient's privacy," I said after I'd taken her aside so no one could listen, "but I think the patient in the bed next to my husband has TB. I'd like my husband moved to another room right away."

The move happened within five minutes—and the roommate turned out not to have TB after all. Maybe I overreacted and maybe I didn't, but my first priority in that situation had to be Michael. What's more, I think one of the qualifications for being a good caregiver is to stick your nose in where it doesn't belong.

CHAPTER 9

Who's the Boss of Me?

- - - - - - - - - - - - -

*"Have 'the talk.' And if you're a patient, make sure the person
you give power of attorney to has your back."*

—KELLI JACKSON, RN, Santa Barbara Cottage Hospital

Michael and I were at the Pasadena office of our attorney several
years ago when she said, "By the way, you two really need advance
directives."

"Huh?" I said articulately.

"Living wills. Durable power of attorney documents,"
she replied.

Michael and I looked at each and shrugged. Not only
did we not know exactly what she was talking about, but
also we weren't the least bit interested in having a discussion
about our options should we become diaper-wearing ninety-
year-olds. We were baby boomers. We had survived Woodstock,
the sexual revolution, and the wearing of truly ugly tie-dyed
clothes. Yes, he had a chronic illness and I had anxiety about

his chronic illness, but we would live forever. Who wants to think about being incapacitated?

Nobody.

We'd all like to believe that if we were ever in an accident or developed a serious illness, we would nevertheless have all our faculties and be fully competent to tell the medical staff about everything from our allergy to penicillin to our aversion to fennel.

When Michael and I balked at the idea of filling out the documents, our attorney said, "Don't you want to be in charge of your own destiny?"

"Yes," we said. "Of course we do."

"Then be smart and take care of business now—while you still can."

"Okay, fine," we said, not wanting to appear as if we were somehow slacking off in our responsibilities as grownups.

Our attorney handed us the forms and told us to go home and fill out all the required fields, then sign them and have them witnessed and notarized.

That night we spread the documents on the kitchen table and educated ourselves. Here's what we learned about all the terminology after doing a little research.

An "advance directive" is a legal document that spells out a person's wishes on the subject of end-of-life health care. Advance directives are divided into two categories: living wills and durable power of attorney documents.

A "living will" lays out a person's specific wishes for end-of-life treatment—from requesting certain procedures to refusing them.

A "durable power of attorney document" allows a person to designate another person (usually a family member) with the right to make those medical decisions in the event the patient can't do so himself.

Together, the two types of advance directives provide the greatest amount of clarity when it comes to how we want to be cared for—to "control our destiny," as my attorney put it.

Michael and I got down to business, asking each other what sort of maneuvers we'd want if we were in the same situation as Terri Schiavo.

"Do you want to be kept alive with a feeding tube?" I asked.

"Do you want the doctors to give you food and water?" he asked.

"Do you want TV cameras to come into your hospital room and shoot footage of you trying to blink your eyes?" I asked.

"Do you want an extreme makeover while you're on all those machines—hair, makeup, the works?" he asked.

Yes, we made a silly game of it, but we ended up with the hard information we needed and it wasn't the slightest bit uncomfortable or upsetting. And we learned things about each other. Michael wanted the full menu of lifesaving measures, while I said I wanted my plug pulled if I broke a nail.

The important thing is that we did the deed, and I urge others to do it too. If you're a caregiver, you may have already been designated as such in your loved one's durable power of attorney document, but that doesn't get you off the hook; you need to designate someone to take care of you, too.

The challenge for caregivers is how to coax our loved ones to actually sit down and sign these documents. If the loved one is an elderly parent, it can be harder than getting him or her to stop driving.

Our attorney, Karen L. Mateer, deals with the problem all the time in her practice, which focuses on wills, trusts, and estates. I asked her to share her knowledge about advance directives—a subject that most people either find numbingly dull or terribly distressing. For me, legal documents are like math—i.e., they make my eyes glaze over.

Jane: *The terminology of the different documents is confusing. "Advance directives," "living wills," and "powers of attorney." How are we supposed to tell what's what?*

Karen: First, I need to be clear that whatever I'm going to say pertains specifically to the state of California. The terms and conditions of these documents can differ by state.

Jane: *Oh, so it's even more confusing than I thought.*

Karen: Not necessarily. Basically all advance directives and powers of attorney are subject to the probate code of the state in which you reside. To be totally correct, one should consult the state law within the state of residence.

Jane: *Getting back to all the terms, why so many?*

Karen: The "living will" term is not really a term of law, but it's in the common parlance. It's describing the person's specific directive course of treatment as well as the treatment they don't want. In the legal community, "advance health-care directives" is sort of the overarching term that's often used to differentiate it from the financial directives. At hospitals, they use either "advance directive" or "living will." And then there's the "five wishes" document.

Jane: *Never heard of that one.*

Karen: It was originally introduced as a Florida-only document, but a national version was created in '98. It combines a living will with a health-care power of attorney and goes through what a person's individual wishes are: I want so-and-so to make care decisions for me when I can't; these are the kinds of treatments I want or don't want; I would like to be kept comfortable in these specific ways (pain management, personal grooming, etc.); I want to be treated at home as opposed to in the hospital; I want somebody to pray at my bedside; I want a memorial but not a funeral; I want my estranged son to know I still love him. It's almost like a personal care document.

Jane: *Do we have this "five wishes" document in California?*

Karen: We do. It currently meets the legal requirements for an advance directive in forty-two states and the District of Columbia. It doesn't in Alabama, Indiana, Kansas, New Hampshire, Ohio, Oregon, Texas, and Utah. You can download the online version at www.agingwithdignity.org.

Jane: *Why do young, healthy people need any of these documents?*

Karen: Unless you have a crystal ball, you don't know when you're going to have an accident or an illness. There's precious little we can control in our lives, but we can have some clarity about what our desires are if something catastrophic does happen. The Terri Schiavo case had people just about standing in line outside my door to get advance directives drafted because that's everybody's worst fear—that there could be a fight over what your wishes really are. The other point is that we don't live in communities with all of our family members. We often don't have close connections with our family. We may only have friends and they're totally useless in terms of trying to help under these circumstances unless they have power of attorney. You can live with somebody for twenty years and you won't have a say in anything unless you're either married or have the advance directive.

Jane: *How legally binding are these documents?*

Karen: A document is only good if people pay attention to it. If they don't pay attention to it, the only value of the document is that you could conceivably go to court to try to enforce it—or, conversely, to contest it.

Jane: *Most hospitals hand out advance directives, and people can download them online. So why should we pay a lawyer to draft them?*

Karen: One advantage is that an attorney can discuss how the documents work and under what circumstances they're valid—like if you're traveling.

Jane: *Are they valid if you're away from home?*

Karen: There's no guarantee they're going to be recognized internationally, but if you're traveling here in the U.S., most states will honor them; it depends on the state. In any case, you should keep a copy of the document with you when you travel or carry a card in your wallet that says you have the document.

Jane: *I would think people would also use an attorney to have help making the decisions in the documents.*

Karen: I think that's one of the biggest reasons. Using an attorney is an opportunity to talk things over with somebody so you're clear about what your decision-making is.

Jane: *How do you broach the subject with clients? It's pretty touchy, isn't it?*

Karen: Chances are by the time somebody has hit their eighties or nineties, they've bumped up against something in the medical establishment, even if it's only trips to the doctor. Or they know somebody who has had something catastrophic. I often use that as the way in. I say, "Look, I know nobody wants to talk about this kind of stuff, but wouldn't it be helpful for everybody to be clear about what your wishes are just in case there's some reason you can't express them?"

Jane: *What's your advice for caregivers when it comes to nudging our loved ones to get these documents drawn up?*

Karen: If you can get them done when everybody is healthy, it's far better than if you're facing a crisis. We all know that our thought processes are a tad impaired under those circumstances.

Jane: *Right, but then what? What should the role of caregiver be if we're given power of attorney?*

Karen: Your duty is to best approximate your loved one's wishes, whatever they are. And if they're counter to your personal wishes, so be it. If you're appointed under the power of attorney, you're merely being the voice for the person who doesn't have a voice. You are not making the decision. You are not supplanting your will for their will. My advice to the caregiver is to do the best you can do. At the end of the day, if the doctors listen to you or don't listen to you, you've done the best you can do by the person. You've honored his or her wishes. You can't give a greater gift to anybody than that.

CHAPTER 10

Getting on the Same Page as that Sister Who Drives You Nuts (and Other Family Matters)

"In the best of circumstances a sibling should be able to say, 'Look, I've always resented you, but let's figure out how we can divide up this labor.' If that's not possible, it's a good idea to get a psychologist or a mediator and really figure out what everyone's role is."

—MICHAEL SEABAUGH, clinical psychologist

Michael hates calling people. It's a quirk, an eccentricity. It's as if he's convinced the phone will ignite and set his hair on fire if he picks it up and dials someone's number, which is why I'm the one who makes the dinner reservations, invites people over, and checks with the gas company to see why the rates went up.

When it comes to calling his sister and two brothers, he's truly pathetic. They're scattered around the country and they don't exactly call him on a regular basis either, but still, it's weird. If he thinks of it, he'll call to wish them a happy birthday, but he never reaches out to them when he's in the throes of a Crohn's flare-up and could really use their support, the consequence being that they're totally unaware of how bad things get around here.

It's not that he doesn't love his sibs; he just comes from a family that doesn't blab to each other about everything and certainly not about anything the least bit unpleasant. As a result, he could be in the hospital, writhing in pain, a tube down his stomach, oxygen up his nose, and yet his phone conversations with them would go like this.

Michael: "How you doing?"

Sibling: "*Great. You?*"

Michael: "Great. How's the weather?"

Get the picture? Part of the problem is that Michael views himself as the big brother and doesn't want to ask for help, drag anyone down, be "a bother."

"They've been watching me be sick all their lives," he explained. "Telling them I'm in pain or in the hospital is basically like crying wolf at this point. They've heard it all before."

"So?" I protested, always lobbying for full disclosure. "Let them hear it again."

All this benign neglect would be none of my business except that I'm Michael's caregiver; even if *he* doesn't want their support, *I* could use it from time to time.

I remember when he was in a New York hospital before we were married. He didn't have health insurance then and the uncertainty over how he would be able to pay for his weeklong stay was only adding to our stress.

"Don't you want me to call your family and tell them what's going on?" I asked.

"No," he said. "I don't want to bother them."

The usual.

I was tired from the commuting back and forth to the hospital, tired from worrying, tired from doing all the heavy lifting.

"Call your siblings," I said during one visit. "Maybe one of them will fly in and spend time with you."

"No," he said.

I tried again the next day—and the day after that. Finally, he agreed to call the sibs. He told them he was in the hospital and from his description you would have thought he was partying in Vegas.

I decided to butt in and stop the madness. I called them myself and said, "Look, your brother is in the hospital, and it's not because he has a hangnail. He's really sick and I think you should know."

My intervention worked. Suddenly, everybody was calling him and expressing concern. Best of all, his brother Mark spent hours researching the insurance situation and discovered that the hospital had a grant for artists and photographers that was designed to cover *all* their medical bills. Talk about a miracle—something we would never have known about if not for Mark, to whom we are forever grateful.

The moral of that story is that family members aren't aware that there's a problem unless you spell it out for them. How can they help if they don't know what's going on? When it comes to my ninety-five-year-old mother, who lives in suburban New York and is experiencing increasing memory loss, I'm very lucky. My sister, Susan, is nearby in Manhattan, while I'm 3,000 miles away in California. She and I are seven years apart in age, but we get along well. We communicate. We're on the same team. We have each other's backs.

While she's been very hands-on, given her proximity to our mother, and is the daughter who's been designated to make medical decisions for Mom if necessary, she doesn't hesitate to include me in decision-making. I never detect even the slightest hint of resentment that I'm not there full time; she seems genuinely happy to see me when I visit. She knows that I'd be on the first plane out if she asked me to be.

I have friends who aren't so fortunate when it comes to which of them is the boss. Sibling rivalries tend to surface when a parent is ill and the competition for Mommy or Daddy's love kicks in all over again. What's more, reasonable people can and do disagree, which is why it's essential that everybody knows which of you is in charge of an elderly parent, grandparent, aunt, or uncle should he or she not be able to function. Who decides what? Who pays for what? Who sits and holds Mom's hand?

Living wills and durable power of attorney documents will make clear which of you has the legal right to oversee your loved one's medical matters, but they don't compel anybody to share costs with you or indicate how long such payments should last.

My friend Deborah Hutchison came up with an ingenious adjunct to advance directives. Collaborating with Judge Lynn Toler from the TV show *Divorce Court*, she wrote a book called *Put It in Writing: Creating Agreements Between Family and Friends*, in which there is an agreement that specifically addresses the issues pertinent to those caring for an aging parent. The book is part of a series Deborah has termed "A Sane Approach to an Emotional Issue." I asked her to elaborate.

....

Jane: *There's a sane approach to being a caregiver? Who knew?*

Deborah: That's the purpose of the agreements: to find the sane approaches.

Jane: *I'm guessing your own experiences as a caregiver led to the aging-parent agreement.*

Deborah: Right. My mother, who had been living on her own, was diagnosed with Alzheimer's and needed to live with me. I'm the oldest child in a family of three siblings and now I had the responsibility of caring for Mom. I said, "Okay, I can't take care of Mom all by myself. I have a sister and brother. How might I split up the responsibilities? How might I have the kind of guidelines that were so helpful in the other agreements in the book? How do we as a family come together and help one another? And let's do it before Mom is in such bad shape and I am so exhausted that those old family dynamics start to come up."

Jane: *The agreement has all sorts of contingencies and charts. How did you figure out what to put in it?*

Deborah: I just talked to people about the different possibilities. For example, maybe Mom and Dad are okay and just need to be looked in on. Maybe they need a little help with groceries and things like that. I offer suggestions about how the siblings can split up the responsibilities.

Then you have parents at the next stage where they can't drive, can't handle their finances, can't see, and can't remember to take their medication. If they're not going into a community and they need help, it's time to sit down with your siblings or get on the phone with them, take a look at the agreement, and make decisions about who will do what.

If you have someone in the family who's astute with finances, give them the financial responsibilities. If you have someone who's more astute with the medical matters, give them the medical responsibilities. If you have someone who is better able to look in and drive them around, give them those responsibilities. The point is that it's a very, very tough thing if one person tries to do it all.

Jane: *How did you and your siblings divvy up the responsibilities?*

Deborah: My sister is a trained nurse, so she has the medical knowledge, and I'm taking care of Mom's overhead. My brother decided to contribute money. And when he can, he'll come out and stay with Mom so my sister and I can have respite and take time away.

Jane: *How do you know everyone will live up to what they said they'd do?*

Deborah: You don't. But once you sign the agreement you're promising to do something, which is a gentle way of making a commitment. Nothing is set in stone. But if you sit down and you make the promise, it's a nice way of coming together and saying, "We've got to do this."

Jane: *Is the agreement legally binding?*

Deborah: No. That's not what this is about. It's more about setting guidelines, communicating, participating.

Jane: *What if the siblings are estranged?*

Deborah: This is not for a completely dysfunctional family, although you can still invite an estranged sister to sign the agreement. If she chooses not to do it, she chooses not to do it. And even if she does choose not to do it, it might bring up things she wouldn't have thought about and she might just take a moment to call her mother or volunteer to help.

Jane: *How should people broach the subject with their siblings?*

Deborah: I recommend that you download the agreement and send it to everybody in the family so you've all read it before discussing it. We have a cover letter that comes with it. It says, "I'd like to invite you into this agreement." And I love the promise, which says, "Let's be prepared to help our parents as they age by working together towards his or her well being and supporting one another in that effort." That's really what it's about: how do we help our parents and support each other—and stay sane during a very emotional time.

For anyone who would like to download Deborah's agreement, visit her website at www.saneapproach.com, go to "Agreements," and click on "The Caring for Our Aging Parents Agreement/Emotional Contract."

Have any of the caregivers in our support group had issues with a sibling over the care of a loved one? Take a look.

➤ **Barbara Blank:** "I'm my father's primary caregiver because I'm the only one here in Florida with him; my siblings are in other states. There's usually one person in the family that has the wherewithal and the strength to do the caregiving, and it seems to be me in this family. But it was always like that. I'm very nurturing and domestic, and I can multitask. My other siblings are caring—it's not that they're not nice—but they just kind of stand on the sidelines and go, 'Oh, isn't that wonderful. Look what she can do.' Do I resent it? Yes. I think it's insane that they don't step up to the plate. Who needs to be asked to help a parent? And if you have to ask, what good is it? I don't ask. I just do it. I do have to say that one of my brothers is a physician and he makes the medical decisions for my father. And although my sister's nickname was 'Queenie' growing up and she's lived up to her name really well, she did step up to the plate when my mom was really sick in California. So maybe it evens out."

➤ **Cecilia Johnston:** "I have a difficult brother, but I've learned to massage him. If there's any little thing going on, I'll call him and say, 'What do you think about this?' And he'll tell me and I'll say, 'Yes, of course,' and then I don't listen. It makes him feel like the big man that I asked his opinion, and I go ahead and do what I think is best. But I do use my brothers to help. When my dad was still driving and shouldn't have been, one of my brothers was flying in to visit. I said, 'You're going to be the one that tells him not to drive because you get to go home.' So I've used my brothers to do my dirty work, which turns out great. It's a good tip for caregivers: use your siblings."

➤ **April Rudin:** "My sister and I are complete opposites. In terms of making decisions about our grandmother, I would say, 'Let's take her out shopping,' and she would say, 'Let's stay here and stare at her in her chair.' One time, after a visit with our grandmother, we were stressed about what was going on. We got on this little commuter flight to go home, had a fight, and just stopped talking to each other. But we loved our grandmother very much and always came together for her. Since my sister was an attorney and I was married to a doctor, she handled all the legal aspects, like drafting the living will, and it was my responsibility to interface with the doctors. She also contributed quite a bit financially.

She and her husband stepped right up to the plate. We didn't have a formal agreement about money; it was just generosity on her part."

Psychotherapist Tina B. Tessina has had plenty of experience counseling siblings around this issue:

"The best thing siblings can do, even if they don't get along, is to let each one do what they do best," she said, echoing what Deborah and others have said. "If somebody is really good with the finances, that person should handle the elderly parent's finances. Maybe someone else can handle the physical care of the parent or, if not, maybe they have a good job and can contribute money toward hiring a professional caregiver. There are going to be siblings that just can't deal with hospitals or nursing homes and you have to accept that. There are going to be siblings that live across the country and you can't force them to do otherwise. Just try to divide up the responsibilities and find a way to let the rest be okay."

And if you can't divide up the responsibilities either because everybody's in a state of anxiety or because you have a sister who doesn't speak to you, take the advice from clinical psychologist Michael Seabaugh: "Get a psychologist or a mediator."

CHAPTER 11

Who Knew Friends Could Be So . . . Unfriendly?

- - - - - - - - - - - - - -

*"I often think that the reason many friends stay away
is because they're afraid this could be their life. You find out who
your true friends are."*

—SUZANNE MINTZ, cofounder, National Family Caregivers Association

"Michael, you got so fat!"

I nearly did a spit take of my white wine when a man Michael and I hadn't seen in a few months blurted out that little gem. I mean what kind of a jerk calls you "fat" right to your face? I kind of choked when he said that, and the wine went up my nose.

We were at a cocktail wedding reception on a sunny Saturday afternoon in Santa Barbara. Michael was going into the hospital for yet another surgery that Monday; he had a partial obstruction and needed a resection. He was on a high dose of prednisone and his face and neck were bloated, but he had pulled himself together so I wouldn't have to go to the party alone.

"I'm not fat," he replied much more good-naturedly than I would have. "It's the steroids. I'm having surgery in a couple of days."

"Hey, good luck with that," the guy said, as if Michael had just told him he was about to go parasailing. He didn't ask what the surgery was for or how long Michael would be in the hospital, nor did he apologize for his crack about the weight. Instead: "Listen, I gotta tell you about the new photography equipment I just bought. It cost a bundle, but I can't wait to take it to Kenya when I fly there in two weeks and . . ." *Blah blah blah.*

I remember thinking, what a huge asshole. This was someone we had once considered a friend? While it was true that the relationship was a casual one as opposed to a bond of longstanding, the overt lack of concern for Michael took my breath away.

Still, I reminded myself that illness is a tricky business. A lot of people are uncomfortable talking about it, being around it, worrying they might catch it, feeling pressure to say just the right thing. There are even those who literally grow weak in the knees whenever medical matters are brought up and will do anything to avoid the subject.

Another complicating factor is that most people don't really understand what's wrong with Michael; Crohn's disease isn't familiar to them unless they have it or know someone who's had it. What's more, he functions like a "normal person" much of the time, so maybe they don't believe he's really *that* sick on those occasions when he is.

And then there's the nature of Crohn's itself; who wants to discuss nausea, bowel obstructions, and explosive diarrhea? Not exactly dinner table conversation.

And yet, why do friends have to disappear just when we need them the most?

About a week after the incident at the wedding reception, I got an e-mail from a woman I admired.

"How are you?" she asked. "It's been awhile. I miss you. What's new?"

"I miss you too, so let's get together," I wrote back. "What's new is that Michael just had surgery for his Crohn's and has been in the hospital four times this year. It's been a rough patch."

Not a word back from her, either in an e-mail or a phone call. Not an "I'm so sorry" or an "Is there anything I can do?" or even a "Give Michael my love"—and certainly not a "Yes, let's get together." Just silence. I ran through all the above excuses; she was uncomfortable talking about illness, didn't understand Crohn's, didn't know what to say. Bottom line? She "missed me" but couldn't bring herself to follow up when I'd told her my husband was in bad shape. She is so off my list now.

I try not to hold grudges or keep score of who was supportive and who dropped us like a brick, but I don't always succeed. It hurts to be dropped. It hurts to have "friends" move away from you as if you carry a stink. It hurts not to have people wrap their arms around you and say, "We're here for you." Intellectually, I get it. Emotionally? Not so much.

On the other side of the spectrum, we've always had a core of close friends who've been nothing but solicitous and supportive when Michael's been ill. They know when to call, when not to call, when to visit, when to back off. They're the people I can count on, and I hope they know they can count on me too.

Has anyone in our caregiver circle experienced the falling away of friends because of a loved one's illness? I asked them.

Their responses are poignant and I appreciate their candor.

➤ **Yudi Bennett:** "Until my son Noah got language, he acted out. We would try and go out with our friends who had typical kids and ours was always the kid throwing the tantrum and everybody would be looking and saying what bad parents we were. So gradually our friends with typical kids stopped calling. It was very hurtful. Even some of our friends with no kids stopped calling. We were all about autism and they didn't want to know from it. I have two friends who have been my friends since I started in the film business forty years ago. They never abandoned us. My family never abandoned us.

"The people who abandoned us were the ones I socialized with after I first had a baby—the friends from Lamaze class and the preschool and the Mommy and Me group. All those people fled, because they were raising their nice healthy babies. Even now, people will call up and say, 'I don't know what to do. My daughter can't decide between Yale and Princeton.' I couldn't even get my son into first grade! The other thing that really pisses me off is when people send me one of those Christmas letters about how wonderful everything is with their family. At the end they'll write, 'Hope you had a wonderful year too!' Don't they look at the person they're addressing these letters to? How insensitive is that?"

➤ **Barbara Blank:** "My husband is very, very hard of hearing, along with having some dementia, so our social life has changed dramatically. We still have couples that are friends and they're wonderful and amazing, but I'm very cognizant of how some friendships have faded. Some people are uncomfortable with the situation and can't handle it. At first I didn't understand it and I took it personally. But my neighbor is a psychologist and she said, "It's not about you. It's about them."

➤ **Harriet Brown:** "There are different layers of what happens. One layer is that when your family is going through a big crisis you sort of pull in. You're not social. You don't go out. And because my daughter's anorexia involved eating, it made me very aware of how many social interactions involve food and we couldn't do any of that for a really long time. So part of it is you're simply not participating. You're out of the loop.

"And then some of it is judgment from other people. One friend said, 'Oh, I could have told you that Kitty had an eating disorder six months ago.' I wanted to strangle her. If that were really true, why didn't she say something to me if she was my friend? And what possible purpose did the comment serve? There were friends that were incredibly generous. But then there were people who just disappeared. They didn't say anything like, 'I can't deal with you and your problems,' but that's pretty much what it was."

➤ **Judy Hartnett:** "When my husband, Paul, was diagnosed with MS, there were friends who said, 'Adios.' I wasn't aware of it right away, but they stopped inviting us. It didn't really hurt, because I figured that if people dropped us, we didn't need them anyway. I still have the people I love, the group I always cared about. What all this allows you to do is *not* do what you don't want to do. That's a freedom that normal people should have. If I don't want to go somewhere, I don't go. I don't have to say why, either. It's liberating."

➤ **Karen Prince:** "After Andy's stroke, his best friend—the man who helped him build a business—never had anything to do with him again. Nothing. His wife would come over and take Andy to therapy for me, but he wanted nothing to do with Andy. I was so angry. I'm still angry. All that the wife said to me about her husband was, 'He just can't handle it.'"

➤ **Toni Sherman:** "About twenty years ago, I was one of the founding members of our book group of about fourteen women. Three of the women were close friends of mine before the book group. The rest were women I liked a lot. We met once a month at each other's home. We also went on trips together, sharing rooms and cooking together and all of that. It was a very warm, congenial, if not loving, group of women.

"When my daughter Courtney got sick and then my mother was dying, I stopped going to the book group and didn't appear there for five or six months. During that entire period not one woman, aside from my three close friends who were hugely supportive, contacted me. Not a phone call. Not an e-mail. Nothing. One of them had been a client of mine for twenty years. And she'd had breast cancer and I had been so close and attentive to her when she was having treatment. She finally called me and said, 'I heard your mother died and I'm so sorry. When are you coming back to book group?' I said, 'I'm not coming back.' She was stunned and asked for an explanation.

"I told her that not one of the women, whose lives I had been such a part of for so long, had made a phone call or sent an e-mail. She started to cry. I said, 'I don't have anything to come back to. The book group, as an intellectual pursuit, really meant nothing to me. What meant so much to me was the communality of the group—the close-knitness of the friendships, the shared intimacies that had gone on for so many years.' I didn't raise my voice. I didn't sound angry. I was just so hurt and I said that. About three days later she wrote me a letter. So did another woman in the group. They were lovely letters, apologetic, not making excuses. I wrote each one back and thanked them for the letters, and I never went back. I couldn't do it."

Stories like the above are all too familiar and give new meaning to the term "fair-weather friend." But psychotherapist Tina B. Tessina thinks we shouldn't be so hard on those who flee.

"Human beings are human beings," she said. "We all have our frailties and failures. Sometimes people just don't know how to deal with illness so they go away. Sometimes they don't show up at the hospital because their mother went to the hospital when they were four and was never seen again. If this friend is important to you, I'd suggest reaching out. Just say something simple. Don't get into 'Why haven't you,' because that produces defensiveness. Just say, 'I'm wondering if there's a way we can get together.'"

Health coach Nancy Kalish recommends that when friends do offer to help we should take them up on it.

"People are dying to help," she said, "but the truth of the matter is they don't know what to say to you. They're going to say very stupid things for the most part like 'Hang in there.' Or they'll tell you about their aunt in Wisconsin who had pancreatic cancer. They're reaching for anything they feel will help. But they also want to help you in other ways—by bringing over food, keeping you company, giving you time to yourself so you can go out while they watch the person. Take advantage of whatever they're offering."

Michael Lindenmayer, founding partner and chairman of the Caregiver Relief Fund, believes that giving fair-weather friends a pass can be good for the soul.

"Just because some people aren't going be there for you in the hard times doesn't mean you have to cut them out forever," he said. "You watch. One day they'll call on you for help, because you're the one who lived it, and then you'll have to tap into compassion or maybe even mercy and forgiveness, and it'll feel surprisingly rewarding."

Maybe. But Michael Lindenmayer makes another point that will not only elicit a laugh but put the responsibility for holding onto our friends squarely on our own shoulders.

"When you leave that house," he said, "don't spew your woe-is-me story because not everyone can handle it and you will get isolated. Don't go around saying, 'Oh, my life sucks. My life sucks.' No one wants to hear that. So if you're going to go watch a movie with a friend, don't walk in saying, 'I can't change another adult diaper!' At least wait until after the popcorn."

My feeling about friends is this: Treasure those people who act on their expressions of concern and let the others go. We know how short life is. We know how important it is to keep stress and negativity at bay. We don't need to dwell on the friends who've disappeared. Goodbye and good luck to them.

CHAPTER 12

Does Working Mean You Don't Care or Does Caring Mean You Don't Work?

- - - - - - - - - - - - - -

"Whatever you have done in your life that awakened your passion or made you feel worthwhile, pick it up again."

—GAIL SHEEHY, *Passages in Caregiving*

I was in the middle of writing a screenplay last spring when Michael needed surgery. My collaborator and I had been on a roll; he would draft a scene and e-mail it to me, and I would draft a scene and e-mail it to him, and we were making great progress toward reaching our targeted deadline. The last thing I wanted was to abandon the script at such a critical juncture and leave him in the lurch in order to sit by Michael's bedside watching him eat Jell-O. At the same time, the last thing I wanted was to leave Michael in the lurch in order to sit at a computer typing: "Cut to."

Writing isn't a hobby for me. It's a job, as well as a passion. I don't dabble in it; I approach it with all the focus, discipline, and seriousness it requires. It's how I express myself. It's part of who I am in the world. It pays the bills and has for a very long time.

I can't just stop doing it for extended periods—especially not when a writing partner is depending on me to hold up my end.

But being at my husband's side when he's having a medical crisis is also who I am, because I love him and wouldn't be anyplace else.

What I'm saying is that I'm like every other caregiver—wracked with guilt no matter what I do. If I'm with Michael, I'm shirking my responsibilities as a writer and breadwinner. If I'm at the computer, I'm a crappy wife and a selfish person. In fact, I can still hear the words of a woman who said to me on the phone, as I was leaving the hospital to go home and resume writing, "He's sick and you're *working?*"

You would have thought I had slaughtered a baby turtle.

What's the balance? How can we as caregivers be at peace with our choices? How do we juggle and feel comfortable about it?

My challenge isn't as difficult as that of those who have nine-to-five jobs, without the luxury of flexible work hours. I'm also my own boss, so there's no one whose permission I need to seek if I have to care for my husband. But I'm no less torn in my twin desires: to be with Michael and to work.

It's when I force myself to stay in the moment that I'm not torn. When I'm with Michael, I say, "Be one hundred percent present, so you can be the best wife and caregiver you can be." When I'm working, I say, "Be one hundred percent present, so you can be at your most creative as a writer." Trying to be in two places at once is a recipe for failure at both ends.

And there are benefits to working even though we give care. Work can be a wonderful distraction from the day-to-day monitoring of our loved one's every ache and pain. It allows us to forget that we've got trouble at home—to lose ourselves in something we're good at as opposed to something we wish we didn't have to deal with in our life. It reminds us that we're more than a nurse/maid/drudge. It's a way to get out of our own head.

Here are some of our other caregivers on the subject of work/care:

➤ **Yudi Bennett:** "I stopped working as an assistant director for periods of time after Noah was diagnosed with autism, but it was my husband, Bob, who totally changed his career by setting up his budgeting business for movies at home. Once Noah started school I did go back to work. It was a welcome distraction. I loved my career. And Noah's therapies were very expensive so I felt like I had to help pay for them.

"When Noah was six, I had just finished a miniseries about the Beach Boys and Bob had been feeling very, very tired. He'd been running low-grade fevers and going to the doctors for months, and they kept testing him for chronic fatigue and other things. Nothing showed up. Bob, unfortunately, was not a good advocate for himself. And I was working around the clock—this is where it was bad that I was working. Finally when I had time off I went to the doctor with Bob and actually raised my voice to the doctor, something I rarely do. I said, 'Look, my husband is not a complainer. If he is telling you he's not feeling well, there must be something wrong and you need to find it.' A couple of weeks later they figured out he had cancer.

"I totally stopped working. Noah was now in first grade so he was in school from eight to two. I flew my niece in from Israel and hired her to be Noah's au pair for the two months that

Bob would be in the hospital. When Bob died, Noah was very autistic. He didn't have age-appropriate language and he had a lot of issues. And then sometime around puberty, he became much better functioning. I wish I knew why, so I could bottle it and give it to everybody. Suddenly he became highly verbal. He'll talk your ear off. So he has exceeded my expectations. There are days when I'm depressed because I gave up my career and a lot of money. But then I remind myself that I doubt Noah would be where he is today if I had continued to work."

➤ **Victor Garber:** "Work was a distraction for me, but I saw my mom as often as I could. For example, I would take her to brunch at Orso's on Sundays, which she loved. We'd sit on the patio and she would see celebrities and she had an amazing recall for them. She always knew before I did who was there. When she was young, she was a singer and a television personality in Canada with her own show. She was very successful when I was a kid—a star in our community. She moved to Los Angeles, both to get away from Canadian winters and to pursue her dream of becoming a television personality and actress. She did get the occasional one line on a sitcom, but that was all. I used to bring her to the set of *Alias*, and she would always ask Jennifer Garner if there were any jobs for her. Jennifer, who was so unbelievably sweet and caring and kind with my mom, would say, 'Yes, Hope. I'm sure there's a job for you here.'"

➤ **Cecilia Johnston:** "I've started a business recently; I'm an educational consultant now. I teach families how to prepare for college and how to go through the whole process of applying and getting in. The job feeds my soul because I'm helping these kids who have their futures in front of them. That helps me because I have been part of the whole dying process for five years, watching both my parents go downhill."

➤ **Jeanne Phillips:** "I began working with Mom when I was a teenager, earning my allowance by answering stacks of mail from other teenagers. In my twenties I wrote the Dear Abby radio show for more than half of the twelve years it was on. And then I got married and lived life. After my divorce, Mom said she needed somebody to do some organizing for her in the office. I ended up working with her for many years, well before she got sick. If she wasn't feeling creative, I'd be creative. If she didn't write copy, I'd write copy. If I read something I thought was off the wall or that didn't seem right to me, I'd fix it. If she couldn't keep her own schedule, I would try to talk to her about it and so would her personal assistant so it wouldn't get screwed up. When she was diagnosed with Alzheimer's, I had been writing the column for a long time. I was already busy but I got busier."

➤ **Suzanne Preisler:** "My sister and I did floral arrangements for years, even while she was getting treatment for ovarian cancer. There were times when some of the drugs she was taking gave her short-term memory loss so I would say, 'Could you cut these flowers this way?' And she'd say, 'Sure.' Two seconds later she'd say, 'What would you like me to do?' Once she finished the chemo and started to get back to normal, she just put the cancer in her rearview mirror and moved on, and we continued to work together."

For those of us in creative fields, "work" can evolve into projects having to do with caregiving. Harriet Brown turned her daughter's struggle with anorexia and her family's strategy for treating the illness into a moving and extremely instructive book.

"I kept an extensive journal," she said. "I'd go down to my office at the end of the day or sometimes during the day and just write down everything I could remember. I knew that someday I would want a record of it, and it really was cathartic."

Suzanne Mintz and Michael Lindenmayer both used their experiences as caregivers to launch national organizations that benefit other caregivers.

Linda Dano became the national spokesperson for the "Caregiver's Survival Initiative" program sponsored by Novartis on behalf of their Alzheimer's drug, Exelon.

"The stats are just extraordinary about how many caregivers also die in this process because it's just the hardest job on the planet," she said. "I really believe I helped people with that campaign, and in doing so I helped myself."

And now, with this book, I've found a way to write about my adventures with Michael—but not before asking him if it was okay to use him "for material." He laughed and said, "You've been doing it for years. What else is new?"

CHAPTER 13

The Home Health-Care Invasion

"It's really important to get as much home care as you possibly can for your loved ones, because that frees you up to have a relationship with them and that's the most important thing."

—TINA B. TESSINA, psychotherapist

Let me begin this chapter by stating unequivocally that I am extremely grateful to the conga line of nurses who came to my house daily to care for Michael after his most recent surgeries. They changed the dressing on his open, gaping, thoroughly nauseating-looking wound (I referred to this daily ritual as stuffing a turkey), checked his vital signs, made sure there was no infection, and performed their duties professionally. Well, except for the one who was hard of hearing and not only spoke *in a really loud voice* but couldn't tell if he was saying "pain" or "vein."

While I valued the expertise of the home health-care workers who were sent by the surgeon to care for Michael and I appreciated the fact that they were the ones poking around in his guts, not me, their visits were, in a word, disruptive. We live in a small house. My office sits right next to the bathroom we had converted into Michael's "infirmary." I couldn't get any writing done while they were conducting their business, which could be any time of day, depending on their schedules. I'd sit at my desk trying to concentrate, but inevitably I'd hear their conversations and roll my eyes in frustration. Once, I put on Bose headphones to block out the noise, but I was so afraid I might be needed and miss a call for help that I took them off after about six seconds.

Having strangers in your home, no matter how well meaning they are, can add to a caregiver's stress even as it relieves it. I'm sorry if that sounds paradoxical, but it's true. Hospice workers are a whole different ballgame, as are those who help with lifting, bathing, and feeding loved ones. I don't know a single caregiver who doesn't view them as angels.

In my case, those who came to our house were both angels *and* invaders.

One nurse wore so much perfume that I had to open all the doors and windows to fumigate the place the minute she left. I was surprised by her lack of sensitivity in this regard; even hospital volunteers are taught not to wear fragrances because they can make patients sick.

Another nurse was a closet smoker. No, she didn't sneak outside to have a cigarette, but she reeked of tobacco and had both a heavy cough and teeth the color of tree bark.

Oh, and then there was the one who suffered from panic attacks. We live up in the hills and our steep, winding road must have triggered her fear of heights. She'd make it all the way up to the house, but spend the first ten minutes of her visit sitting in a chair hyperventilating.

The best nurse was the hard-of-hearing one. She showed up when she said she would and had a kindly, maternal manner. There was just her loud voice, which grew into an actual shriek during one very memorable visit.

I was sitting at my desk, making an effort to write at least a page or two, when I heard this: "*Oh my God!*"

"What's going on?" I called out.

"*Come quick!*" she cried. "*It looks like a tennis ball!*"

A tennis ball?

I leapt out of my chair and ran to Michael. He was standing up, his bandages off, looking pale and shaken. The nurse was freaking out and could hardly speak. She motioned me closer, pointed to Michael's incision, and said apoplectically, "*I don't know what that is!*" She was so shaken up I couldn't decide whether to hug her or slap her.

I peered at Michael's belly and, sure enough, there was a round pink object protruding from his wound. Since the nurse was still speechless, Michael called the surgeon and described what he saw to the doctor's nurse.

"Sounds like it's a section of your colon," she said. "Have your wife bring you in right away."

We hopped into the ambulette, and Michael was back in surgery within the hour. It's not every day that one of your husband's organs nearly falls out of his abdomen, so I'm not pretending I was cool and calm about it all—especially when

I found out that the medical term for what happened is such a lovely word: "evisceration." But I was a lot less hysterical than the nurse whose job it was to come to our house and look after him.

It's not easy when your house is suddenly not your own—no longer your sanctuary but rather a mini-hospital with the smells and sounds to match. What's the best way for us to handle outsiders who take us away from our normal routine, even as they provide an invaluable service? How can we stop feeling intruded upon and embrace our new reality?

What I did was to rewire my way of thinking about home care. Instead of focusing on the irritating characteristics of the people who came to help, I focused on the help itself—on the fact that I was damn lucky to have that doorbell ring and find someone standing there who knew how to change bandages and spot a pink tennis ball popping out of an incision. So what if I was inconvenienced? They were *there*. And they reminded me that I needed to let go of having to run the show—that caregiving is also about delegating.

I asked our caregivers if they had any encounters with home-care workers of any sort and, if so, whether the experience was positive or negative:

➤ **Victor Garber:** "After my mother was diagnosed with Alzheimer's and could no longer function on her own, there were the caregivers from the Jewish Family Health Service or whatever it was called. They would send people over, and we set up the system of having someone come in during the day so she would have company and someone who could drive her. That went on for a while. It was a disaster because most of these people were paid nothing and they were incompetent. It was one person after another.

"Finally, I found the caregiver that basically saved our lives. She was remarkable and has become a friend. She said she would work for my mom for a month or two and then she fell in love with her and stayed for five years. She had looked after children, not people with Alzheimer's, but she was instinctive and bright and a very special kind of person. She had great empathy for my mother. I actually believe she kept her going longer."

➤ **John Goodman:** "I met a nurse's aide in the hospital. She freelanced there, and my wife, Donna, kind of got attached to her. I asked her if she'd come home with us when Donna was discharged and she said yes. She was living in our house and was so helpful. There was a lot of 'women's stuff' and bathroom stuff that would have been very difficult for me to deal with. She really helped get me through those initial weeks. Now she's like part of the family. She went to my daughter's wedding."

➤ **Judy Hartnett:** "Paul is completely not able to transfer, which means he can't move himself from the bed to the chair or get on or off a toilet. He hasn't walked in years. He has use of his left arm, but his right side is useless. I used to do all the lifting myself, but a car accident two years ago has done me in. Now we have help as much as I can afford. One aide was a pothead—a complete stoner—but I didn't care if she was a heroin addict as long as she showed up and took good care of Paul. And then there are the hospice people, who are all incredible. They really like what they do and sincerely want to help."

➤ **Suzanne Mintz:** "My husband has the progressive kind of MS so he's in a wheelchair full time and has limited use of one arm and hardly anything functional on the other side. We have help twice a week in the evenings. The person comes and gets him into bed, helps him in the middle of the night if he needs it, and gets him up, showered, and dressed, and gives him breakfast in the morning. He's on his own during the day. He's got a Lifeline buzzer in case there's an emergency, and he's got a power wheelchair so he gets around, and he's got his computer and lunch is made. When I travel we have to put together arrangements as well. Not being able to delegate binds you to caregiving. Some things can get done without you, and you have to separate out the things you really think are your province."

➤ **Jeanne Phillips:** "There was always a housekeeper living at the house with my mother, so it wasn't like I was carrying bedpans. I know from others who are experiencing Alzheimer's that there does come a time when somebody must live with that person because they are no longer able to take care of themselves, particularly if there should be an emergency. Some families go into denial. When the family member is difficult to deal with, no one wants to accept it. I was lucky. There have always been excellent people taking care of my mother. They are angels on earth."

➤ **Karen Prince:** "When Andy came home after months in rehab, he couldn't talk or read or write. His right leg was weak, but the left leg worked well and he could walk with a cane. I had a caregiver come in three days a week to shower him and make sure he had his breakfast and lunch. He could put something in the microwave, so on the days when I went to work I had the microwave set for a specific time, and I put stickers all over it that he understood. Or I'd have something in the refrigerator and it would have a dot on it so he'd know it was for lunch. We came up with a way of communicating with each other, so we didn't need that much outside help."

➤ **Harold Schwartz:** "My son Joseph had an incredible caregiver. Actually, he had two people. One was a fellow who worked afternoons-to-evenings five days a week—a very skilled medical worker. Then we put an ad in the paper and this amazing man answered the ad. He was independently wealthy. He had retired in his early fifties and just wanted to do something good for somebody. He was incredibly close with Joseph. He ran the household. After Joseph died, he signed up with the ALS Association in Washington and now they give him people to work with."

Getting help is key, even for us caregivers who think we have superhuman powers and can do it all. It's that need for help that propelled businessman Michael Lindenmayer to start a Chicago-based venture called the Caregiver Relief Fund. This is a man who was living in Brazil, having a great time in great weather, involved in a myriad of other pursuits. What did he know about caregiving or the need for "relief"? I asked him to enlighten me.

....

Jane: *You could have put money into any sort of enterprise. Why did you pick this one?*

Michael: It all started when I came back to a small town in Michigan for a brief visit to see my grandfather, who was nearly ninety. He'd been living with my parents for the last twelve years. When I arrived I did not recognize any of them. They were so distraught in the worst way possible, every single one of them.

Jane: *Distraught, as in sick, or very upset?*

Michael: My grandfather was on fifteen-plus medications. He had emphysema and he bled a lot—almost like a hemophiliac. He wasn't one of those fountain-of-youth ninety-year-olds; he was in decline and in total denial about it. My father was overweight and had never been that way before. He had migraine headaches every other day. My mother is one of those people who stayed calm even in the most extraordinary circumstances, but she was not that way anymore. She had become a full-on, every-single-day caregiver and it had taken its toll.

Jane: *Did they try to get home care to help out?*

Michael: Yes, but when I asked that question my mother started crying. She said, "The woman showed up in hot pants." I said, "Okay, but there must be another person." She said, "There was another person and she showed up and started grumbling about her tooth-ache, so I took her to the dentist. A third one showed up and she had hot pants on too. I asked her why she wasn't wearing a uniform. She said, 'My washing machine broke.' The woman came back and brought six loads of laundry and I said, 'I can't have this craziness.'" So I saw all this during my visit, and my weekend became a week, which became a month, which became a year. I became a caregiver to all three of them because I realized that the situation wasn't going to improve unless I stepped up to the plate and helped.

Jane: *But helping your family is one thing. Starting a fund to help the rest of us is another.*

Michael: Having become a caregiver, I started to see how crazy making it was. I stood back and looked at America and said, "This is absolutely terrifying. This nation has done zero to prepare itself for something that is inevitable."

Jane: *You mean the fact that the population is full of sick people?*

Michael: I mean that at some point, someone will need to be the caregiver and someone will need to be the care receiver—no matter who you are. In the U.S. we have spent billions and billions of dollars trying to live forever and now we do. But it's a be-careful-what-you-wish-for story. We have medical patients and we have aging people, but we totally took the caregiver out of the equation.

Jane: *So you decided to do something about it.*

Michael: I became morally moved. I felt that if I could help promote a mainstream view toward caregiving, have it be something that is viewed as positive and that needs to be addressed on a very practical basis by each family, then I'd be making a significant contribution to the culture. So I set up the Caregiver Relief Fund.

Jane: *For those of us who've never started a fund, which is probably most of us, how did you go about doing it?*

Michael: I called the CEOs of some of the largest at-home care agencies and I said, "I would like you to donate part of your marketing budget to vouchers that I will then give away." The idea was that the at-home agencies would send the vouchers, and a nonmedical-care person would come to your house and give you four hours of respite.

Jane: *Nonmedical. So we're not talking about a nurse or aide.*

Michael: No, these people don't do the medical part, but they can do a million other things for you. They may run errands or keep your family member company or do whatever needs to be done in the house.

Jane: *Why four hours? Is that just an arbitrary number?*

Michael: Four hours is just enough time to get people familiar with what the service is—and to recognize that they are exhausted. Anyone who's been at it for a year or longer and takes even four hours off can actually say, "Oh my gosh. I didn't realize I needed help." So it's a provocation to get them toward the second part, which is planning. We encourage them to plan.

Jane: *For what?*

Michael: For at-home care. Most people, even low-income people if they're smart about how they spend their money, can afford some amount of at-home support. But some people have never had exposure to staff or service of that kind and there are misconceptions like "Only rich people have servants." So just getting them exposed to at-home care is a big cultural shift because if they don't get help they'll burn themselves out doing things they're unable to do. And once you have a caregiver down for the count, you've doubled or tripled your expenses.

Jane: *Are these vouchers available to people in every state?*

Michael: We work with over six hundred locations across eleven states. We'll get full national coverage in the very near future.

Jane: *What do applicants have to do to be considered for these vouchers?*

Michael: They should go to our website at www.caregiverrelieffund.org. They'll find out how to move forward with an application. We review all the applications and prioritize them. Then we connect the applicants with the at-home care agency in their area and they will schedule amongst themselves when the care will be done. The four hours can be used all at once or for one hour each week for four weeks. It's up to them.

Jane: *What do most caregivers do with those four hours of free time?*

Michael: Usually, the first thing they do is cry. Caregivers very rarely are recognized, so it's like being given an award that says, "I recognize how hard you're working." After they cry, they either keep doing more caregiving, because they're codependent and can't help themselves, or they get a haircut.

Jane: *A haircut? Seriously?*

Michael: There are a lot of people walking around with a mop on their head because they haven't had a haircut in a year.

Jane: *I'm guessing most applicants are women?*

Michael: Yes, but it's not as imbalanced as you would expect. More and more men are recognizing that they're caregivers. If you look at the health studies out there, they've found that caregiving is bad for both men and women, but it's actually worse for men. They often delay telling people about the situation even longer than women, because they think they should be able to handle it. I'm a guy so hopefully I'm validating this for them, saying it's okay to admit you need help. I've taken on all kinds of challenges in my life and never shied away from one. But this caregiving journey nearly crushed me. It literally took me to a pulp.

Jane: *How's your family doing now?*

Michael: My grandfather passed away, but my family got healthy while he was still alive. We went from worst-case scenario where I think my parents were on the verge of divorce, my father was about to have a heart attack, and my mother was in a severe depression, to a family that united. The process of going through this really helps you understand who is important in your life. And it makes you realize just how short this ride is and how you better do something cool with it.

CHAPTER 14

Using the *F* Word, as in *Facility*

- - - - - - - - - - - - - -

"Placing someone in a care facility very often turns out to be the best solution for everybody. The caregiver can stop changing diapers and just relate to the person who needs care, allowing them both to spend quality time together and make a few more memories."

—TINA B. TESSINA, psychotherapist

My ninety-five-year-old mother is a smoking-hot chick. She has an eighty-eight-year-old boyfriend, walks a mile a day on a treadmill, and is an enthusiastic member of her monthly book group. Until recently she was still zipping around in her Subaru—the sporty model with a spoiler. She's in remarkably good physical health (knock on wood), but her memory began to falter a few years ago and I didn't see it coming, nor was I prepared to modify my own behavior accordingly.

I was staying at her house during a weeklong visit, and we were talking about the Yankees, our favorite baseball team.

I said, "Remember the time I was in the city with Michael and we ran into Scott Proctor on Fifth Avenue?" Scott Proctor was then a Yankees relief pitcher.

"Michael wasn't there," my mother said matter-of-factly. "You and I were in the city together when we saw Scott Proctor."

"No," I said. "Michael was with me, Mom. I was in the city to meet with my publisher."

"*I* was with you that day," she insisted. "We had lunch."

Instead of recognizing her confusion and leaving the subject alone, I kept it going, motivated by the need to be right. "You and I haven't been in the city for lunch in years," I said. "I was there that day with Michael."

Her expression darkened. "So you're telling me I've lost my marbles, is that it?"

It dawned on me in that moment that my mother, who had always been so sharp, hadn't lost her marbles but was having a memory lapse.

At first I wrote off the episode with: "Well, she's in her nineties. Give her a break." But as time went on, it became clear that she wasn't just getting the specifics of events mixed up and forgetting names; she was repeating questions she'd asked only minutes before and becoming disoriented when there was too much information thrown at her at once. The fact was that despite her youthful appearance and her ability to not only laugh at herself but also to skillfully cover up her memory problems in social situations, her lifestyle needed to change. The question was how? And who would make her change it?

She was resistant to any kind of meddling by her "jailers," as she referred to my sister and me. She wouldn't give up the keys to the car, wouldn't wear a Life Alert necklace, and wouldn't have anybody come and live with her, despite the fact that her house is on seven acres at the end of a private road with a driveway so steep even the deer want no part of it. And she absolutely, positively refused to go into a facility for seniors or, as she put it, "one of those places."

But then she did an about-face. Some of her friends and relatives had sold their houses and moved to an imposing complex in Westchester, so the idea suddenly seemed acceptable to her. The community offers every conceivable type of residence and boasts a full array of cultural amenities and dining options. My sister and I set about trying to make the move happen for Mom. We were relieved that we would no longer have to try to convince her that her days of living alone were over.

I did some research and found an organization that handles such moves on a regular basis—a group of experienced women who come to the client's house, sort through years of clothes and furniture and knickknacks, measure the new space versus the old space, and help to figure out what to give away or sell and what to bring.

After a couple of visits with my mother, these women could see that she wasn't up to the task. The whole process of moving— or, more accurately, of confronting a change in her environment— overwhelmed her.

It was time to go to Plan B: find her a live-in companion.

Of course, Mom hated that idea—I mean, seriously nixed it.

"I am *not* having a stranger live in this house following me around!" she'd say over and over. "I need my privacy. And I don't need a nurse!"

She didn't need a nurse, but she did need someone to drive, shop, cook, accompany her to doctor's appointments, make sure she took her medications, keep her from feeling isolated and lonely.

We stayed on her about hiring a companion, and eventually wore her down with: "Do you want to fall and break your hip and be stuck here for days all by yourself?"

My sister and brother-in-law interviewed several candidates and were thrilled when they met Sandy, who had experience as a professional caregiver, came with terrific references, and spoke in a lilting Trinidadian accent that was as upbeat as her personality.

Mom couldn't help but fall in love with Sandy, and the two of them have been living happily ever after since the day they were introduced. Thanks to Sandy, my mother is healthy and well cared for in her own house. They go shopping, have lunch with Mom's friends, take trips, even visit Mom's boyfriend together at the assisted-living facility where he now lives.

For other elderly parents, staying in the house with a live-in caregiver might not be an affordable option or even the best one. And for some seniors, particularly those with dementia, a facility is often a necessity.

Still, there are many caregivers who try to compromise by keeping their loved one at home and taking advantage of adult day-care centers like the Friendship Center here in Santa Barbara.

"The Friendship Center was started in 1976 by a group of social advocates who saw a need in the community to have supervised care for the aging during the day so caregivers could have a respite," said Heidi Holly, the center's executive director. "We're finding that more and more adult children are caring for their relatives at home—the sandwich generation of baby boomers who have children and are taking care of their elder parents. Our government needs to do something about this burgeoning situation of baby boomers living longer. It's going to be, as they say, 'the silver tsunami.'"

The Friendship Center is open from eight a.m. until five p.m. They not only have buses that pick up their members around the city but they provide meals, administer medication, and offer activities that keep the members engaged.

"And we're affordable," said Heidi. "So many caregivers have a fear of the unknown when it comes to their finances. They'll say, 'What am I going to do about Mom next? Live-in facilities can run $8,000 to $10,000 a month! I'll be broke!' We work with people, so they pay what they can."

Sounds like a good deal to me, although I'm not sure my mother would have agreed to go if she'd been living with one of her children.

"When older people are hesitant, I say come and hang out and try it for a day," said Heidi. "Have lunch and meet some of our members. What's key is the socialization. Studies have been done where people who stay socially engaged are happier."

The Friendship Center and other adult day-care facilities provide an invaluable service for their communities and, of course, for caregivers—a fabulous option.

As I said, I'm lucky my mom is living comfortably at home, but if she couldn't manage adult day care and it became necessary for her to go to "one of those places," how would I deal with the guilt of removing her from familiar surroundings and sending her off to live with a bunch of strangers? How would I deal with the realization that the move would be her last stop? I pride myself on facing reality, but the whole notion of placing a parent in a facility when he or she desperately doesn't want to go makes me want to crawl into a hole and hide.

I reached out to my caregiver support group to see what their experiences have been.

➤ **Barbara Blank:** "My father just moved into a community. Right now it's independent living but there's assisted living in the same complex if he needs it. I had been bringing home brochures about this place, because we all knew the time was here, but he was resisting. I would make appointments there and he would cancel them. The day we were going over to sign the papers was very traumatic for him. He said, 'I'd rather go to the cemetery.' I said, 'Okay. Get in the car and we'll go to the cemetery then.' He looked up and smiled. I was calling his bluff and the humor brought him back.

"Ultimately, it was his decision to move. His eyes were getting bad and he had fallen a couple of times, and he realized that his balance wasn't right. He sold his car himself; he knows he can't drive anymore. He's still very bright and functional. He takes his own medicine. He makes his coffee. He has a martini every day at four thirty. But now he'll be in an environment that's safer, where he'll get fed and where he'll have maid service every week."

➤ **Linda Dano:** "I got my father placed at Mary Manning Walsh, a Catholic nursing home in New York. The only bed they had available was in the women's ward. So he was surrounded by women for his entire two-and-a-half-year stay there. Some little old thing, who also had Alzheimer's, saddled over to him and they became a couple. My mother was okay about it. She was happy someone would sit with him. When she got dementia, I hired a caregiver for her and bought her the apartment next to mine. Eventually, I took her out of New York and put her in a lovely nursing home in Connecticut and she flourished there before she started to go downhill."

➤ **Victor Garber:** "At a certain point my mother couldn't stay in her apartment, so I started looking around for a facility. That was a depressing proposition—just to go around and see what's available. I couldn't imagine putting her in the places I saw. They were overcrowded and there's that smell when you walk in. Unless you have a lot of money it's pretty bleak.

"I was in a more fortunate position and I never took that for granted. I settled on Belmont Village in Los Angeles. It was a new facility and I passed it on my way to work every day. One day I just went in and looked at it and I thought, this is it. I got her a really beautiful two-room apartment with a view. For the most part, Belmont Village worked out very well. My mom loved to sing, and karaoke was a community activity in the main sitting area. She would get up and sing and everyone's mouths would drop because she had a beautiful voice."

➤ **Cecilia Johnston:** "I remember my mom and I were sitting at Thanksgiving and she was talking about a friend who lived at the

Samarkand in Santa Barbara and this friend had invited Mom to lunch there. She said to me, 'Wouldn't it be wonderful to live someplace where you never have to cook again?' I could just see the light bulb go off in her head. The next thing I knew she was on the Internet and signed up for the Samarkand. She and my father have lived there since 2000. They have levels of care and we've gone through all of them at this point—from independent living to skilled nursing. The best gift my parents have ever given me was to move to the Samarkand on their own. It took so much of that burden away from me. But it's been a big adjustment.

"You know how everybody says, 'I wish my child came with a manual?' I wish my parents came with a manual. You don't know what's going to come down the pike."

➤ **Cissy Ross:** "With me there really was no choice about moving my mother to the Samarkand. She had been kicked out of her assisted-living place in Florida because they said she needed too much care. My sister had offered to take her in New York, but I felt it was easier for me to have her here in California. I was in graduate school and had a more flexible schedule. My mother was extremely businesslike about it. And she was trusting in our judgment—not thrilled but practical."

➤ **Diane Sylvester:** "I brought my mother up to Santa Barbara from Los Angeles to live at the Samarkand. In the beginning she was in assisted living there and was fairly independent. She could walk and take care of herself and eat at the dining table. We had Thanksgivings and Christmases with her there, and it was nice.

The situation deteriorated when she started to fall and had to move into skilled nursing, where she was for three years before she died. It worked out well. I feel like I was given the last couple of years with my mom. They were beautiful years. So all the hell I went through was worth it."

➤ **Jackie Walsh:** "About five years after my father passed away, my mother was diagnosed with macular degeneration. She called me one day and said, 'Jackie, I've made a decision. I'm not going to drive anymore. If a child ran out in the street, could I stop fast enough? No.' She never got into the car after that and she lost a lot of her independence.

"It was her choice to move to the Samarkand. At first she was in her own apartment in independent living. As her eyesight diminished she had an apartment but with a full-time nurse on staff. On her ninety-fifth birthday, she was getting all ready to go out for lunch and she slipped, fell, broke her hip, and ended up in skilled nursing. She was there for three years until she had a stroke and lived about a week. But moving there was always her choice."

Clearly, with our aging population in this country, care communities are the wave of the future. Michael and I don't have kids, so someone will have to take care of us when we get really old and decrepit. Will that "someone" be a parade of paid staff members at a nursing home? I figured I'd better ask a person who runs "one of those places" what I can expect in case I'm shipped off with or without my husband. I interviewed Elizabeth Schierer, director of assisted living and memory support at Maravilla, a seniors' facility in Santa Barbara.

Jane: *How many patients do you have at your facility?*

Elizabeth: Patients? Never use that word. They're residents.

Jane: *Sorry. How many* residents *do you have?*

Elizabeth: I think it's somewhere in excess of 350. And we are not a facility—that's the F word. Never say that either.

Jane: *What's the correct way to describe Maravilla then?*

Elizabeth: We're a community. We have the pleasure of working in the residents' homes. That's the thought process.

Jane: *What's the social life like? Do the residents get along with each other?*

Elizabeth: In general they do. But there can be cliques.

Jane: *You mean like in the movie* Mean Girls?

Elizabeth: Exactly. In the dining room, people go, "Why are you sitting at my table in my seat?" Or "Why are you wearing that today?" It's just like high school only more exaggerated. There are bullies I have to deal with.

Jane: *There's bullying at a seniors' community?*

Elizabeth: Oh, yeah. And we have people that hoard food. Or maybe they like to "shop" in the laundry room and accidentally wear women's underwear. You get everything—even sex.

Jane: *Come on!*

Elizabeth: I had a ninety-nine-year-old man who wanted to meet with me to talk about the fact that one of the female residents wanted to sleep in the apartment with him. He was asking my permission.

Jane: *As if you were his mother. What did you say?*

Elizabeth: I said, "Well, you're ninety-nine years old and if she's consenting and the family is aware then go for it."

Jane: *You mentioned his family. Do you get much interference from family members?*

Elizabeth: It's really annoying when we have something in place because it's what's best for the residents and a family member will say, "I've been on WebMD and they say it should be this way." Suddenly they assume the role of expert and don't listen to us. Also annoying is when a family member wants a laundry list of things for the caregivers to get done. "Make sure there isn't one Kleenex dropped on the apartment floor. Make sure the shades are open this amount. Make sure the TV is set on this channel." But there's such guilt among family members around the issue of moving their loved one here.

Jane: *How does the guilt manifest itself?*

Elizabeth: A lot of phone calls and some overinvolvement. There's a real separation anxiety at first. The interesting thing is that within a month or two it's gone. The residents are happy and the family is happy, and life goes on.

Jane: *What if you get a really difficult family member? How do you deal with him/her?*

Elizabeth: You always listen to family first because there's no doctor or caregiver who knows the person better than the family. And then you try to work within the boundaries and compromise.

Jane: *Do you mind the complaints?*

Elizabeth: No. My mantra to my staff is "When we know better, we do better." But there's a way to complain. Don't start out yelling. Take a breath and then be specific and realistic. And remember: I'm so on your team.

Jane: *You said there's a lot of guilt with family members. I would imagine there's denial too.*

Elizabeth: Absolutely. I have a physician whose mother lives in the community. She has dementia. She needs to be transported to my memory-care unit, but I can't get this professional physician to do it. His answer is, "I'll have to check with her and see how she feels." She doesn't remember how she feels from one minute to the next! There's all this resistance because he doesn't want to think of his parent that way. There's nothing I can do unless it gets to the point where I decide it's a safety issue.

Jane: *So people don't want to believe their parent has dementia?*

Elizabeth: No, they don't. They'll move their loved one into our community and say, "You lost my mother's dentures." It could be that one of the other residents with dementia wandered into the apartment and flushed them down the toilet. That happened. The toilet was overflowing and we called maintenance and they said, "We found someone's uppers."

Jane: *I'm trying and failing not to laugh at that.*

Elizabeth: You have to have a sense of humor about the denial. I once went to the home of a highly respected surgeon, because his family asked me to do an assessment. They said, "We think he might need assisted living." Mind you, they'd told me he'd gotten in the car and driven to another state and that law enforcement had to get him and bring him back. I was there for the interview and he said, "Have you met my wife?" I said, "No, I haven't had the pleasure." I knew that his wife was dead, but I went with it. He said, "Oh, here she is now." This black cat walks into the room. I said to the cat, "It's very nice to meet you." I thought, this family isn't sure if he needs assisted living? The black cat was kind of a defining moment for them.

Jane: *What would help ease the transition for family members?*

Elizabeth: I really think that things would go more easily if they had more educational support. I was sitting with a resident recently. She said, "I've been here about two years and I like it. However, when I moved in, my children decided what I should have in the apartment.

They sent along twelve crystal goblets that I've never used, but they didn't send along the photos I loved." The move wasn't empowering for her because she didn't get to choose her own things. Even if there's trepidation about moving a parent in, family members need to let him or her be part of the process.

Jane: *Any other advice?*

Elizabeth: The best advice I can give is to get their parents or grandparents in before they are too far along in their decline cognitively, so they can adjust to the environment, make friends, jell. Don't wait for the crisis. Don't wait until you're at the end of your rope. Don't wait for the black cat moment. And stop being afraid that it'll happen to you next.

CHAPTER 15

Finding a Shoulder— or Ten—to Lean On

- - - - - - - - - - - - - -

*"We don't have family. We don't have community.
It's lonely out there. Create a family of other caregivers."*
—NEAL MAZER, psychiatrist

In the early years of my marriage to Michael, it seemed that everyone with a disease or a condition or a syndrome was joining a support group. He asked his gastroenterologist if he should go to a group for Crohn's and the doctor said, "Don't bother. Nobody wants to sit in a room and talk about their bowels. Too embarrassing."

Michael gave up on the idea until he saw an announcement for a Crohn's support group in our local newspaper.

"I think I'll go," he said. "Do you want to come?"

"Me?" I had zero interest. My mother believed that sharing medical stories (or problems of any kind, for that matter) with anyone other than family and close friends was unseemly, that it carried the whiff of complaining; that it was best to put on a brave face and give the world the impression that everything was fine. Besides, why would I want to spend any more time dwelling on Michael's Crohn's than I absolutely had to? "No thanks," I said. "But I think it'll be great for you to go."

Michael went to the support group and continued to go one night a month for a year. Since he had Crohn's the longest of anyone there, he became the group's leader and ended up giving more support than he got. He felt good about helping others, particularly those who had just been diagnosed and had no idea what to expect. They thought their lives were over, but Michael was living proof that they could have careers, marriages, whatever they wanted.

His most poignant interaction was with a thirteen-year-old girl who came to the group with her mother. The girl was suicidal, a complete mess. Why? Because her teacher at school wouldn't let her go to the bathroom during class and she would soil herself as a result, not to mention get routinely teased by the other kids.

Michael was so incensed on her behalf that he called the principal of her school and said, "Do you realize that what you're doing is criminal? This child wants to commit suicide and if she does it'll be on your watch."

The principal was very apologetic—she hadn't known anything about it—and promised to rectify the situation.

Clearly, there's value in attending a support group, and as a caregiver I should have understood that. But every time I thought about reaching out to others, I said, "I'm too busy. I don't need to swap sob stories. I'll feel better when Michael feels better."

Now I get it, thanks to the people I've met through this book, some of whom experienced the benefits of support groups firsthand, like Cecilia Johnston, Cissy Ross, Diane Sylvester, and Jackie Walsh, who met because they each had a parent living at the Samarkand community. They bonded and formed a support group with several other women that they call "The Daughters of Samarkand," and the group has evolved into one of enduring friendship. (Other caregivers take note: That "daughter" you keep running into at your parent's new home just might become your BFF.) Here's how they found support from one another:

➤ **Jackie:** "I was getting ready to leave after a visit with my mother. As I turned the corner where the elevators are, I saw a woman named Angie sitting on a bench crying her heart out. I sat down and put my arm around her. One thing led to another and we ended up laughing. The director walked by and said, 'Is everything okay?' All we could do was sit there and laugh and cry at the same time. We said how much we had enjoyed our encounter and being able to laugh about the sad things. The director said, 'There used to be a family group. Would you two like to see it started again?' We said absolutely. She put the chaplain in charge and we started the group."

➤ **Cecilia:** "The chaplain arranged for our meetings, but we would still meet even if she couldn't be there. And once a month we would have a luncheon with our moms in one of the private dining rooms."

➤ **Diane:** "We're super-duper best friends who don't feel obligated to have to keep in touch every second."

➤ **Jackie:** "If one of us saw something that we did not like, we were not shy about addressing it. If we said there should be little vases of flowers on the table at lunch or cloth napkins to make the atmosphere more cheerful, we were listened to."

➤ **Cecilia:** "And if there was an aide that did something we didn't like, we'd share the information with each other and then usually one of us or a couple of us would go and talk to whoever was in charge. We didn't want to be a problem. We wanted to be the solution."

➤ **Cissy:** "It's a very profound experience to be running your parent's life, so being part of 'The Daughters' was important to me. In addition to liking them, I liked their mothers. I would have gone crazy without the others. It just made it like normal life instead of some abyss."

➤ **Cecilia:** "And there's a comfort that somebody else knows your mom, can pop in on her, make sure everything's okay, and report back."

➤ **Jackie:** "My husband was extremely supportive, but having a parent in a facility isn't something you want to go home and talk about every evening. With 'The Daughters,' we could talk about it every day and we're still talking about it. So I think it was good for our marriages to have 'The Daughters.'"

And "The Daughters" are not alone in their praise of sharing.

➤ **Victor Garber:** "My brother, who was caring for my father while I was caring for my mother, went to a support group and he said it was life changing. When you go to a program where you hear another person's story and it resonates with you, you just feel less alone and helpless."

➤ **Michael Lindenmayer:** "When you have other people who are going through what you're going through, you can laugh together and say, 'Oh my gosh, this is just so absurd.' Most caregivers curl up in an isolated cocoon, cut off from the planet. But if you outreach, you'll meet other everyday angels or heroes who are really loving and caring, and it'll be amazing."

➤ **Karen Prince:** "I recommend support groups highly. Even after Andy's death, I'm still a member of the stroke support group. At first I wasn't happy about going; I used to take those two hours and read somewhere by myself. But going to the group was the best thing I ever did."

Alternative-medicine practitioner Martha Rolls Collins believes there are health benefits to attending a support group:

"If caregivers don't have somebody to talk to, if they're not keeping a journal, if they're not getting the words out of their body, the stress is going to be stored energetically and it's going to affect their breathing patterns and their body posture and their ability to function. They'll get flooded with the emotional experience of what's happening and there will be health consequences.

So they need to join a support group—just to be able to verbalize out loud to other people who are having an experience similar enough to theirs that they won't feel judged. Then the emotion gets processed instead of being stored."

Psychiatrist Neal Mazer agrees that support groups are important for a caregiver's well-being, but adds that we should do more than vent.

"Support groups have to begin by being places where you can dump your pain," he said. "But once that's done, you've got to move on and say, 'Okay, what skills do I need? How do I take the next step?' It's about developing your strength. It's about crying and saying, 'Why me,' and then moving quickly into growth and saying, 'What am I learning?'"

What I've learned is that my mother was right about many things when I was growing up, but she was wrong about keeping problems to myself; that there's a great deal to be gained by revealing that my world is not perfect.

CHAPTER 16

"Caregiver Sleep" Doesn't Have to Be an Oxymoron

- - - - - - - - - - - - -

"During sleep your body stops pumping out cortisol, the stress hormone, so it gets some relief, which is why a good night's sleep is so important for good health."

—NANCY KALISH, certified health coach

Sleep is a beautiful thing. I love everything about it—from slipping between clean, cool sheets to sinking into a state of complete restfulness. I love reading myself to sleep. I love reaching up to turn out the light. I love the moments in the dark just before drifting off. I love dreaming. Come to think of it, there's nothing I don't love about sleep except that I have such trouble doing it.

I'd never been a great sleeper under the best of circumstances, and menopause turned me into a card-carrying insomniac. But throw a sick husband into the mix? Forget about it. Whenever Michael was in the hospital, there was almost no point in going to bed at all. I'd obsess about everything that could conceivably go wrong with him. I'd run through the list of all the tasks I had to accomplish the next day. I'd beat myself up for being the sort of hyper person who couldn't just roll over and nod off.

A glass of wine would make me drowsy enough to get to sleep, but I couldn't *stay* asleep. By two a.m., I was wide awake, heart pounding, looking over at the empty space in the bed next to me, wondering if everything was okay at the hospital, feeling an overwhelming sense of anxiety and loneliness.

I'd change positions, prop myself up with another pillow, try thinking happy, relaxing thoughts. I'd turn on the light and dive back into the book I was reading. I'd watch some television. Nothing worked. By morning I'd be a disaster, walking into walls and feeling like a slug.

"Get a prescription for Ambien," said a friend.

I got a prescription for Ambien. It knocked me out for three hours, tops, and gave me a gnarly hangover.

"Try Benadryl," said another friend.

I tried Benadryl, as well as Tylenol PM and Advil PM and every other PM on the market, along with Nyquil. They did help me sleep but they also sucked all the moisture out of my head and gave me a case of cotton-ball brain.

"How about a prescription for Valium?" a third friend chimed in. "Or maybe Xanax."

I was already a Xanax aficionado; a doctor had prescribed it years ago when I was about to appear on the *Today* show to promote my first novel. As a former publicist at several New York publishing houses, I was more accustomed to remaining behind the scenes, promoting other writers, than to being in the limelight myself. But now I'd written a book and it was my turn in front of the camera, and I was so freaked out that I took two Xanaxes before I went on the air instead of one. When the segment began, Katie Couric said, "So, Jane, how does it feel going from being a promoter of authors to being an author yourself?" I felt my eyes roll back in my head and I said, "I don't know. I'm heavily sedated." Katie laughed and the interview continued, but I cringe every time I relive that day (even though the story has gotten a lot of mileage on the author-speaking circuit).

The point is, I knew that Xanax was short acting and, therefore, not strong enough for a full night's sleep—not for me, anyway. And Valium? By that time, I was so not interested in becoming a pill junkie.

I did hit on one solution while I was flipping through a Brookstone catalog. I spotted an ad for a white-noise machine called Tranquil Moments Sleep Sound Therapy and bought the machine on the spot. It comes with twelve sounds—from "rain" to "ocean surf." The digital recordings play over and over again and are intended to lull you into a state of relaxation that leads to sleep. I'm sure that most people use machines like mine to block out disturbing noise. (I live in the hills of Santa Barbara; the only "noise" I hear is dead silence.) But I've found that "ocean surf" does relax me. It even makes me drowsy and I recommend it to my fellow caregivers-insomniacs. Does it work on those nights when my mind is really racing and I'm convinced a sumo wrestler is standing on my chest? No.

Luckily, certified health coach Nancy Kalish shared her advice for eliminating those endless, torturous hours of tossing and turn-ing. I've tried all her suggestions and they're extremely effective.

The one I find foolproof is No. 5, although I use a heating pad instead of a hot-water bottle. The sensation of the heat on my belly has a truly soporific effect and I go right to sleep—a blessing.

NANCY KALISH'S SLEEP TIPS

* Resist the urge to do any napping during the day. Sometimes people grab catnaps, but that really cannibalizes your sleep; very few of us can get away with anything longer than a twenty-minute nap during the day and actually go to sleep at night.

* Remove yourself from all sources of light. That means the computer screen and the TV screen, as well as lamps. Light prevents the release of melatonin, the hormone that allows you to fall asleep. Studies have shown that even nightlights keep you up.

* Go outside during the day. Your first morning exposure to sunlight is key to your sleep later that evening because it resets your body clock to normalize your function. If you're inside all the time because you have to take care of someone, you are wreaking havoc on your body clock. Even if you can't get out during most of the day, it's really important to get out first thing in the morning—for even fifteen or twenty minutes—if you want to sleep well that night.

* Invest in a sleep mask for your eyes. If you live in an area—say, a large city—where there's a lot of light coming in through your windows, a sleep mask makes you feel almost like you're in your own little isolation tank.

＊ Get an old-fashioned, red rubber–designed hot-water bottle. I know it sounds really retro and silly, but I use one and it really does work. A heating pad is okay too, but the hot-water bottle is even lower tech and easier to use—no cords or plugs—and it's only about fourteen dollars at the local drug store. Just fill it up with really hot water and place it on your stomach. It calms you down. It helps with digestion. It soothes you into sleep.

＊ Spray your pillow with a lavender oil spray. It won't put you into a dead sleep right away, but it has a very relaxing effect. You could also try an herb pillow, which is like a sachet but filled with herbs, the primary one of which is lavender. Having the lavender on your bed is better than bathing in it, because the scent won't dissipate and you want it near your nose when you go to sleep.

＊ Count backward from one hundred. This one is really tried and true if your mind is racing with a zillion thoughts. It's a variation on counting sheep. It calms your breathing but also quiets your mind and gets your brainwaves to stop spiking. You can't obsess about what you have to do the next day if you're focused on counting. And if you lose your place, you just go back to wherever you thought your place was, so there's no fretting.

CHAPTER 17

The Great Escape— Taking a Mental Vacation

"Any time you can get to escape will refresh you.
It really helps you keep your mental and emotional balance."

—TINA B. TESSINA, psychotherapist

The other night—just after a friend called and asked, "How is everything?" and I said, "Fine"—Michael informed me that he needed to go to the emergency room.

"What now?" I said with a combination of concern and resignation. It was, of course, the July Fourth weekend. Why should there be a holiday without a trip to the ER?

"My toe is infected," he said, showing me the offending digit, which was red and swollen.

Since my husband now has peripheral neuropathy on top of his Crohn's (he can't feel his fingers and toes), he's not supposed to go barefoot; if he bumps a toe on the leg of a chair he won't feel it, and a bruise or break could turn into an infection. The upshot is that he didn't listen to the doctor, and the result was yet another anxious holiday weekend instead of one spent frolicking with non-sick humans.

At the ER, Michael was given an antibiotic that caused him to hurl for most of the weekend, while I kept thinking back to those old commercials for Calgon bath soap. Remember them? The ones where the woman has had it with the kids, the traffic, the demands of her life, and she looks up in exasperation and says, "Calgon, take me away"?

Sadly for the advertising agency that came up with the campaign, what takes *me* away isn't a soak in the tub. But I do have my go-to methods of escaping—of focusing on something entirely unrelated to medical problems. Brain breaks are essential for caregivers, whether that means withdrawing into a movie or throwing ourselves into a new hobby. The objective is to relieve the stress—if only for an hour or two.

I have a friend whose distraction of choice is any Lifetime movie featuring a woman in jeopardy; she revels in the fact that the heroine's predicament is always worse than her own. Another friend gets away from it all by reading real estate listings online and fantasizing about properties with gazebos and wine cellars and guest cottages over garages. Still another friend knits scarves; she's made so many she could wrap the necks of the entire population of Rhode Island.

When I need a distraction, I watch Yankees games if it's baseball season, although I expend far too much energy cheering or cursing, depending on the outcome, and wind up exhausted.

For a more relaxing pastime, I go straight to the Food Network, which is another way of saying I'm mad about food porn. There's something about watching professional chefs create dishes I would never dream of cooking that completely transports me out of my reality. Take Ina Garten, the star of *Barefoot Contessa*. Is she not the most calming person who ever stepped in front of the camera? She wears the same who-cares blue blouse-with-the-collar-turned-up on almost every show, speaks softly, doesn't insult the viewer's intelligence, and seems to genuinely like her husband whenever he puts in an appearance. Watching her make scones in the beautifully appointed kitchen of her house in East Hampton is better than taking a Valium. And Giada DeLaurentiis? Have you ever seen a smile like that? She's the happiest damn woman who ever lived. Who wouldn't relax watching her whip up pasta for her equally happy family and friends?

Some caregivers have told me that they cope by performing mindless tasks—cleaning the house, doing laundry, organizing closets—and I can certainly understand why. After feeling helpless for hours, it's satisfying to come home and regain a sense of order and control. The important thing is to do *something*—anything to take your mind off the fact that you've got a kid, spouse, or parent who's depending on you.

Well, not anything, obviously. There are healthy escapes and not-so-healthy ones, and we have to know the difference or we'll sink faster than the people we're supposed to prop up.

I asked some of our caregivers for ways that they've coped during their loved one's medical crisis—for better or worse:

➤ **Yudi Bennett:** "In 1998, before Bob was diagnosed with cancer, we got together in somebody's living room with four other families who had kids with autism and we started a group called the Foothill Autism Alliance. Bob became president and was president until he died. When he was in the hospital having the bone barrow transplant, he had his computer and wrote a 400-page resource guide on autism. It became the bible for all these families. For Bob, running the group was a gift. I think it kept him going and, by extension, me too."

➤ **Barbara Blank:** "I get my hair done at the beauty shop. Even just sitting down for an hour and having my hair blown dry is delicious."

➤ **Linda Dano:** "My favorite escape is always gardening. I get lost in it. And my dogs have been everything to me. They're just there with those little faces and those little licks."

➤ **Judy Hartnett:** "I watch *The Housewives of Atlanta* or any of those housewives. That's my lowest of the low; I may as well be in bed with a box of Cracker Jacks. My sister says, 'Do you actually watch those shows? What's the appeal?' I think it's because my life is so ridiculous that I can watch something ridiculous."

➤ **Cecilia Johnston:** "A couple of glasses of wine help. And I read a lot. I have a Nook and I think I've read 140 books on it."

➤ **Suzanne Mintz:** "My circumstance is different because my work and my personal life are both about caregiving, so it's hard to get away from all of it. I love getting engrossed in a book. Going and getting a haircut is nice. I get massages. And I get manicures regularly. Those are things I do for myself, although my manicurist says I'm the only one she has to tell to relax my fingers."

➤ **Jeanne Phillips:** "I have been blessed with the most supportive husband in the world. He's wonderful. He is my rock. I can talk to him about anything. If I need advice, he'll give me advice. If I need his arms around me, he's always ready. He's helped me to be there for my mother."

➤ **Suzanne Preisler:** "When I was a kid my father used to build a lot of things for my mother, who was Japanese, and I always helped him. So I started building shoji doors just to keep myself occupied when my sister got sick. And I watched baseball like a lunatic. My husband, Jerome, loves the Yankees, but I got the MLB package and would watch any game. It was a big escape for me. And you know how houses in New England have those rock walls? When I thought my mother was going to die, I worked off my stress by building one around our property in Maine—all by myself. I'm 115 pounds on a good day, but I was like Superman lifting up a car."

➤ **April Rudin:** "I escaped into food and alcohol, and my sister shunned both. The only thing we came together on was shopping. We went to some great outlet malls while we were visiting our grandmother."

➤ **Toni Sherman:** "I had a facial once a month, a manicure once a week, a pedicure every two weeks, and a massage once a week.

I was not neglecting myself, obviously. And I had Don, my partner of twenty-four years. He cooked. He cleaned. He marketed. He slid in with all the things that I was not able to do."

Health coach Nancy Kalish has another suggestion for us: listening to music.

"Mozart really does do something to your brainwaves," she told me. "It evens them out, reduces stress, and initiates the relaxation response. If you don't like classical music, listen to anything that gives you pleasure. Also, putting on some music and dancing is helpful, even if it's while you're doing housework or it's only for five minutes. I encourage people to try things even if they don't think they're going to work."

April and Cecilia both mentioned alcohol, and I'm glad they did. I love red wine. Nothing helps me escape the way a glass of Syrah does, not even Ina Garten. Luckily, I never need more than a few sips to feel my muscles relax. I stick to one glass, tops, because any more than that gives me a headache.

So how much escape is too much? Where do we draw the line between healthy escapes and unhealthy ones? What's the difference between a distraction and a dependency?

Linda Dano admits that during the crisis with her father, she wasn't able to tell the difference and, even if she could, she didn't care.

"I kept getting fatter," she said. "I'd finish taping *Another World*, leave the studio, stop at the McDonald's drive-through, get the Big Mac, the fries, and the malt, and then I'd come home and make dinner for my husband and my mother and eat that too. I was abusing myself big time. I was so guilty about giving my father the feeding tube that I was punishing myself."

Michael Lindenmayer reports that there's another, even more insidious, type of behavior that's becoming common among caregivers.

"I'm talking about the widespread abuse of the medicine cabinet of their elder loved one," he said. "That aged person is getting dosed either with some kind of happy pill or sedation, and we're seeing more and more caregivers helping themselves to what's there. Then they'll go back to the pharmacy and say, 'Oh, my father ran out of this prescription early.' And the pharmacist will say, 'How did that happen?' And they'll say, 'I guess Dad went through his pills twice as fast as he should have.' The pharmacist will say, 'Okay, we'll refill it this time.' And then it happens again and again, and what you get are strung-out caregivers."

Clinical psychologist Michael Seabaugh offers simple guidelines for those who aren't sure whether they're escaping or self-medicating when it comes to wine, the favored alcoholic beverage for so many of us.

What's Healthy?
A glass or two that brings down your anxiety and tension levels

What's Not Healthy?
A glass or two that numbs your self-awareness and causes you to do self-destructive things (like finishing the bottle)

I think we all know when we're crossing a line—and that when we do cross it we won't be able to care for anybody, much less ourselves.

CHAPTER 18

Being a Crybaby Isn't Necessarily a Bad Thing

- - - - - - - - - - - - - -

"Generally speaking, crying is good. It's a release of tension and a clear expression of an internal feeling. It can be very healing."

—MICHAEL SEABAUGH, clinical psychologist

After Michael's last surgery following an intestinal obstruction, one of his doctors maneuvered me outside his hospital room and left me with an ominous warning about my husband: "At his age and with all the resections he's had, he really can't have another one."

"Can't have another what?" I said, not playing dumb but wanting him to spell out exactly what he meant.

"Another resection," he said. "He loses more small intestine with each one."

"I thought there was plenty to go around," I said. "Don't we all have about twenty feet of it?"

"You and I do. Michael doesn't. Not anymore. His life is . . . compromised."

My heart dropped when he said that. I wasn't crazy about the little pause in the sentence either.

"His life isn't compromised," I said defensively. "He deals with his Crohn's like a hero. He goes sailing, takes walks with me, has a social life, doesn't—"

"I'm talking about short bowel syndrome," he interrupted. "As Crohn's patients lose more and more small intestine, their ability to absorb nutrients decreases. Certain locations of the small intestine are responsible for absorption of nutrients, vitamins, and minerals."

"So you mean he would need to take vitamins?"

"No. I mean that he would need injections, because the mechanism for absorption by mouth is missing. And, eventually, he would need TPN."

"No idea what that is," I said with dread. It's not a good sign when your doctor uses initials to describe a treatment, at least not in my experience. It's even worse when he uses the initials after the word "eventually."

"Total parenteral nutrition," he explained. "Essentially, it's a feeding tube."

I had no reaction. Zero. I stood there as if he had just recited his grocery list. After a beat or two, I finally let his words register and managed, "He would need this permanently?"

"Yes, permanently. You can't grow new intestine once it's gone."

I did an imitation of a wax figure as he went on to explain that TPN is administered through a battery-powered IV pump and that most patients dispense it themselves, with the help of a caregiver, during several hours at night—forever.

I thanked the doctor for his time. And then, since Michael was sleeping, I went outside to the parking lot, got in my car, and cried for about twenty minutes. No one was parked on either side of me—I had the area pretty much to myself—so I didn't have to worry about turning down the volume on my wails or containing the flow of snot pouring out of my nose. I just sat there and sobbed my guts out. I allowed myself to think lots of poor-Michael/poor-me thoughts, momentous and trivial—from how dramatically his life would change to how much of a crimp a permanent feeding tube would put in my dinner parties. Crying was incredibly cathartic, and my car was the perfect place to do it—a small, confined space that felt very womblike and safe. And I was proud of myself for not melting down in front of the doctor or, more importantly, Michael, as I would have in the old days. As I wrote earlier in this book, I've learned how and when to freak out.

After awhile, I reminded myself that there was no guarantee that Michael would ever need this TPN thing, that the doctor was only projecting into the future, that my catastrophizing wasn't productive, that my husband wasn't dying, only recovering from his latest surgical adventure, that others have it far worse than he/I did.

I pulled a wad of tissues from my purse, mopped my face, reapplied my lipstick, and got out of the car, ready to be perky and upbeat and caregiverish when I walked back into that hospital room.

Crying has been like a time-out for me over the course of Michael's flare-ups and I'm a big advocate of it. I don't do it often, but it does have its charms. I don't love the puffy, red eyes that come with it or the blotchy complexion, but I've found it to be a remarkably effective way to vent my frustration and express my fears. It also allows me to rededicate myself to my marriage and whatever challenges lie ahead because once I've cried, I'm done with the self-pity and I gear up for the next course of action.

Is it healthy to cry? Or am I just a big whiner? I asked Martha Rolls Collins, who practices alternative medicine and mind-body therapies, for her take.

"I have a client who's addicted to crying," she said. "In her case it's a stop sign: Don't come any closer. There are also people that cry because they can't figure out the specific emotion they're feeling. They cry when they're sad. They cry when they're angry. They cry when they're happy. It's all the same thing to them. So the crying needs some focus. You need to realize that you can feel sad without disintegrating. Then you can have a heartfelt, strong connection with the sick person you love. It's very empowering to feel even the greatest sadness and know you'll be okay."

I think Martha's right: crying is empowering, as contradictory as it sounds. That's why I feel better after a good cry. Not only have I released pent-up emotion, but also I've processed whatever the new information is and decided I can live with it, which is no small thing.

So I say do it. Just make sure you've got those little packets of Kleenex and you're good to go.

CHAPTER 19

Sometimes Laughter Isn't the Best Medicine— It's the Only Medicine

- - - - - - - - - - - - -

"Research shows that laughing lowers cortisol levels and provokes a relaxation response. Even faking or forcing your laughter does the same thing."

—NANCY KALISH, certified health coach

I went to the hospital to visit Michael before one of his surgeries and when I got there he was sitting up in bed, his hands clasped together, his brow furrowed, his expression that of someone deep in thought. I stood in the doorway, not wanting to intrude on his quiet time. Was he contemplating his mortality? Reflecting on his life as a person with a chronic illness? Worrying that the surgery might not go well? Whatever it was, I was sure it was something profound.

I waited another minute or two and then walked into his room. I sat beside him on the bed, stroked his forehead, and said, "Are you upset, sweetheart?" I rarely call him sweetheart—we have other, far more juvenile, terms of endearment for each other—

but I was trying to sound mature, like someone who could listen to his insights without snickering.

"No," he said. "I'm not upset."

"Nervous?"

"No."

"Pensive?"

"No."

"Then what?"

"Mortified."

"Mortified? About what?"

"About what just happened."

As I've said elsewhere in this book, my husband doesn't make it easy to have a conversation.

"Okay," I said, reminding myself to be patient. "What just happened? Maybe I can help."

"Too late," he said. "The damage has been done."

"It can't be that bad," I consoled him. "Tell me."

After a heavy sigh, he explained that a nurse had just come to shave his pubic area, as is standard operating procedure prior to abdominal surgery.

"She was really pretty," he said, lowering his eyes.

"And?" I said, waiting for the "mortifying" part.

"And I got an erection while she was doing it," he said. "She flicked my dick with a pen to make it go down. I guess it happens a lot with men and that's how they handle it."

My jaw dropped. This nurse was a dominatrix.

"And did it go down?" I asked.

"Yeah. But the whole thing was really embarrassing."

My first instinct was to say something soothing to my husband, because he really did seem rattled. My second reaction was to be jealous that he'd sprung a boner in the presence of a woman other than me. And my third impulse—the one that prevailed—was to make a joke out of the whole thing.

"At least you can still get it up," I said and laughed at the absurdity of it all. Michael laughed too, and before we knew it we had turned an incident that had made him feel uncomfortable into a story we would later retell whenever we needed a good giggle.

Humor has always been my salvation. When I was growing up in a family of squabbling stepsiblings, there was often tension at the dinner table. I tried to diffuse it by telling jokes. And if my jokes didn't work, I did impersonations of the mailman, the guy at the dry cleaner, our teachers, you name it—anything to get a laugh and prevent somebody from bolting from the table in a huff.

Humor keeps me balanced. Humor reminds me that life holds moments of joy, despite the obstacles we face. Humor is the best antidepressant any pharmaceutical company could ever have invented. I once got a fan letter from a therapist. She said she'd read all my novels and prescribed them to her depressed patients because the stories were "better than Prozac." I saved that letter because it reinforced my belief that humor does get us through the tough times. Black humor, gallows humor, bathroom humor, wry humor—it's all good if it gives us a break from our problems.

Humor is especially important for caregivers; we need to laugh or we'll explode. For me, it's all about comedy—from *Some Like It Hot* to *Bridesmaids*, from *I Love Lucy* to *Seinfeld*, from Nora Ephron to Tina Fey.

It's virtually impossible to hold two thoughts in our head at the same time, so if we replace our sad/anxious/woe-is-me thoughts with funny, lighthearted ones, we're in business.

"A movie or a sitcom is the way to go for caregivers," said health coach Nancy Kalish. "Even if you don't think it'll be funny, watch it anyway because it's still better than not watching. A little bit of humorous distraction really does help."

Best of all, though, are the humorous moments that aren't fiction—the ones we witness in the course of caring for a loved one. It's a gift to be able to turn even the dark times into those that provide laughs, and we all have it in us.

I asked some of the members of our roundtable if they'd ever found humor in their travails, and the answer was a resounding yes.

➤ **Yudi Bennett:** "At one point Noah was mad at me and he slammed the door, wrote a note, put it on the door, and told me I was never to talk to him for the rest of his life. Another parent would have been upset, but I was so happy. First of all he wrote a note, spelled everything right, and it was grammatically correct. And then there was the fact that he expressed his feelings. This was a kid who was nonverbal! Another time Noah told me, 'Get a life, Mom.' He used to talk in this very stilted way, like an Israeli who didn't speak English. Now he was using slang! I celebrate those moments even though some other parent would have said, 'Apologize' or 'Don't be fresh.' I thought, what an accomplishment."

➤ **Barbara Blank:** "My father was walking the other day and my husband went to hold his hand because there was a curb. My father said to him, 'Don't get close to me. People will think that we're gay.' We had a good laugh about that one."

➤ **Harriet Brown:** "After Kitty's first day back at school, she came home with some friends and I was making them milkshakes and she made a joke: 'Yeah, we know all the ice creams that have the most calories. Ha-ha.' I thought it was funny and she thought it was funny and no one else thought it was funny. And then much, much later, we had an experience, again with ice cream, in front of the ice cream freezer at the store, looking for the ice creams with the most calories and realizing that everyone was staring at us in a horrified, disapproving way. We found that hysterical. It so epitomizes what you have to do with this illness and how it goes against the mainstream idea of eating."

➤ **Linda Dano:** "We would laugh because my mother would say the damnedest things like, 'Why didn't you bring the little boy here?' I'd say, 'Well, he was sleeping.' She'd say, 'The one in the closet?' I'd say, 'Yes, that's the one.' My husband, Frank, would get crazy and try to get her to remember things correctly, but I kept saying, 'Make her happy. If she thinks there's a little boy floating around, who cares?' And I found humor all the time with Frank. I was convinced that he shouldn't look like a skinny, gray cancer patient, so I kept feeding him and myself, and we got fatter and fatter and fatter. When he died and I put him in a casket before I cremated him, I had to have the funeral director cut the back of his Armani suit because he was too frigging fat to fit in it."

➤ **Jennifer DuBois:** "My mom eventually needed a walker to get around. That was a tough time because it really demonstrated how much she was losing the fight—the cancer and chemo and radiation were taking their toll. So we got her a walker from hospice, and she and my dad immediately dubbed it 'Johnny,' as in Johnny Walker. Whenever we would go somewhere, she would say: 'Don't forget to bring Johnny with us.' Or 'Where's Johnny?' It was obviously her way—and ours—of coping with the fact that she now needed to use a walker without her having to say, 'I need my walker.'"

➤ **John Goodman:** "The things that my wife said in the hospital made us laugh. She would look at our son-in-law, who was a little overweight, and say, 'You're a big fat pig.' Or she'd look at our daughters and say, 'You're so ugly.' We knew it wasn't her. It was just something in her body making her physically and mentally crazy."

➤ **Judy Hartnett:** "One example is when I took Paul to the doctor's office for a checkup. He's terrified of being cold, so he had a blanket around him from his legs to his waist and a large sweat-shirt with a hood that went over his glasses, and all you could see was his mouth. We went to sign in at the reception desk and I wrote: 'Judy Hartnett and E.T.' The receptionist saved it and it's still hanging on their wall."

➤ **Jeanne Phillips:** "My mother and I would go to the restroom together when we were in restaurants—two girls going to powder our noses—but it became essential that I go with her when she got Alzheimer's. I remember one night we were at a restaurant in West Hollywood. We had gone to the restroom and on the way back to our table she walked ahead of me. There were five or six men sitting at the bar. As we passed, she looked over at them and said loudly, 'Oh, what good-looking men.' Their heads swiveled toward us. None of them was over forty-five, and when they saw who had said it, they didn't know how to react because Mom was in her eighties. I quickened my pace and I announced to them, 'You know, my mother always did have a great eye for good-looking men.' At which point she turned to me and said loudly, 'Don't say I'm your mother. Tell them I'm your sister.' She was a pistol."

➤ **Suzanne Preisler:** "My mother was doing pretty well after starting chemo, but at one point she had bladder problems and had to have those pads on the bed. I should mention that she was the kind of person who would not use a cane or a walker and did not want anybody to know there was anything wrong. So we went to Walmart. My mother sat in the prescription department with everybody else and I went to the counter and said to some kid, 'Where do you have the pads?' He said, 'I don't know what you mean' and yelled out, 'Sandy? Can you help this lady with some pads?' Sandy said, 'You don't mean the underpants?' I said, 'No, I mean the pads.' She said, 'I don't know if we have the pads,' and yelled, 'Lucy? This lady over here in the blue sweater needs the pee pads.' Finally Lucy came back with these little pads. I said, 'I'm not housebreaking a puppy here.' My mother started to laugh. And then she began to tell everybody in Walmart, 'My daughter—she's always been like that.' It was like a comedy routine.

"Also, when my sister was in the hospital, she was supposed to have their chicken broth, which was full of salt. There was a chicken place nearby that has the best chicken soup. My husband, Jerome, was coming to meet me at the hospital, so I said to him,

'Do you have your briefcase with you?' He said yes. I said, 'Go get some chicken soup, put it in your briefcase, and bring it.' He snuck it into the hospital, and we got my sister to eat it. Sometimes when you have those surgeries, they do not let you go home unless you pass gas. I said to her, 'Eat this soup. It'll help you pass gas.' She wolfed down the soup, and Jerome kept sneaking it in there. Sure enough it worked. When she finally passed gas, we were jumping up and down and high-fiving."

➤ **Karen Prince:** "Andy couldn't talk, but he would try to explain things to me as best he could by drawing or using pictures. If I still couldn't get it, rather than get frustrated, he would just throw up his hands, and we'd laugh and forget about it. Laughing is important. Don't push, just laugh, and think of a different way to try later."

➤ **April Rudin:** "One time my sister took our grandmother shopping at T.J. Maxx and my grandmother went to the bathroom. My sister started looking through the racks and forgot about my grandmother. She searched the store and couldn't find her. It turned out my grandmother was locked in a stall and finally crawled out from underneath. She may have had Alzheimer's, but she was resourceful, and she always made us laugh."

➤ **Harold Schwartz:** "When my wife got Parkinson's, I had to cook for her—even though I know as much about cooking as you know about flying a shuttle to the moon. If you can't microwave it, I don't eat it. One time she said, 'I'd like to have fish sticks.' I went shopping and bought frozen fish sticks and put them in the freezer.

The night she wanted them I went to the freezer and took out the fish sticks and saw they were not microwavable. I threw them back into the freezer and said, 'What else do you want?' Also, my wife had to write out instructions for how to use the dishwasher and the washer and dryer, because I'd never done it. She once told me she needed a new lint trap for the dryer. I didn't even know what a lint trap was. And, of course, my son Joseph had an incredible sense of humor. He drank Ensure through the feeding tube, and I'd say, 'What flavor do you like?' and we'd kid around about it."

➤ **John Shore:** "My dad and I went to CVS to exchange his Depends for a smaller size and buy some denture cream. He was shuffling around with his cane, and I couldn't believe this was the same man that used to blow college basketball kids off the court. As soon as we were out the door of the drug store, he started complaining that there was something wrong with the receipt, and all the people were idiots trying to rip him off. He stood right in front of those double doors fumbling around with the receipt and his cane and his glasses, and a crowd started to form because he was blocking the entrance. Inside I was cracking up. I think you have to look for the absurdity of the moment because it's all we have sometimes."

So, yes, laughter is possible even when the situation is bleak. But can you ever laugh *too* hard? Michael did.

He was in his hospital room recovering from surgery and decided to distract himself from the pain in his belly by turning on the TV. He found a channel that was showing an old Laurel and Hardy movie and he settled in. He started laughing and couldn't stop, and the laughter was absolutely killing his newly repaired abdomen. He had to turn off the TV or he'd pass out. Unfortunately, the TV remote had slipped out of his hand and was now dangling between the bars of the bed, out of his reach. He couldn't call the nurse, since the call button was also on the remote. He was stuck trying *not* to laugh until an aide finally came and rescued him.

What did I do when he told me that story? I laughed, naturally.

CHAPTER 20

Just Breathe.
Or Meditate. Or Both.

- - - - - - - - - - - - -

*"Meditation becomes like a best friend to you. It's a
sanctuary, a place you can go to and be peaceful."*
—DEB SHAPIRO, meditation teacher and author

"Where are you going?" I asked Michael one evening a few years
ago. He was standing in front of the bathroom mirror trimming
his beard so it wouldn't look like an out-of-control Brillo pad—
an act he performs whenever he's about to engage with anybody
other than me.

"A meditation class," he said. "Everybody tells me it would
be healthy for me."

"Everybody tells me the same thing," I said, "but I'm just
no good at it. I try to 'still my mind' or however they put it, and
instead I obsess about all the things I should be doing instead of
sitting there thinking about nothing."

"I really want to learn," he said, as his clipping scissors sent
wiry little gray hairs into the sink.

"Good luck," I said. "At least you'll be well groomed."

A few hours later he came home all excited—as radiant and dewy-eyed as a new bride.

"How'd it go?" I asked. "Were there a lot of men with ponytails?"

He nodded. "Women too. And they burned incense. It was really cool."

He handed me a piece of paper with a lot of octagonal shapes on it and explained that while he sat cross-legged on the floor and listened to music in which there were chimes and chants, he was told to focus his mind on the shapes.

"And it worked?" I said.

"It did," he said. "I kind of went into a trance and it was very relaxing."

"I'm jealous," I said. "I'll go with you next time."

There was no "next time." Michael tried to practice his new meditation techniques at home and couldn't recapture the magic of that first lesson. He decided it was all nonsense and gave it up.

Then came 2010 and his four hospitalizations. I'm not sure I took a real breath during that entire year. Well, of course I did. I must have. But I was constantly reacting to crises or trying not to react to crises, running from one task to another, functioning without stopping, gasping for air. I knew I should sit and breathe in that way people who meditate always tell you to, but I didn't—partly because I didn't know the "right" way to breathe. Was my mouth supposed to be open when I inhaled and closed when I exhaled? Or was it the other way around? Was it the lungs that filled up with air or the diaphragm? And what about thoughts while I breathed:

Should I have any? Was it possible not to have any? It all seemed too complicated, and the last thing I needed was complicated.

I wished for the hundredth time that I knew how to meditate, since I kept hearing how much calmer I'd feel if I did. Wasn't it the key to happiness for Elizabeth Gilbert in *Eat Pray Love*? If she could do it, why couldn't I?

I sat on the floor one night and tried. I closed my eyes, took breaths, and said the word "peace" over and over. The good news is that I didn't hyperventilate. The bad news is that my mind quickly veered off from "peace" to "I forgot to empty the dishwasher" and "The air conditioning guy is coming at three thirty tomorrow afternoon" and "Would I have a crush on Justin Bieber if I were a teenage girl?"

I got up and felt like a failure.

Months later I started writing this book and vowed to consult experts on the subject of meditation, especially after two of the members of our caregiver roundtable endorsed it.

➤ **Victor Garber:** "My sister and I were driving in LA one day and she said, 'I'm really worried about you.' I said, 'Why?' She said, 'You're so angry.' I didn't realize it until she said it, but I was angry at my mother's disease and what was happening to her, and I was not able to express it. She noticed it because when I was driving, I would get furious in the car in a way that was completely irrational. So I studied Transcendental Meditation and it helped. I recommend it highly. Take fifteen minutes a day and just allow yourself to breathe. It does have a cumulative effect, so I was able to go through the day with less stress and anger."

➤ **Michael Lindenmayer:** "I meditate in the beginning of the morning, because I don't want to carry any garbage into my day. There are a million different permutations of meditation, but the most basic is to sit down for twenty minutes, breathe, and clear your mind. If you can't take twenty minutes, you should be looking at yourself in the mirror and saying, 'What is keeping my brain so busy that I can't even do that?'"

One of the permutations, I've learned, is what's called "mindfulness meditation," and clinical psychologist Michael Seabaugh is an advocate.

"Mindfulness-based psychotherapy is very big now," he said. "It's really about being in the present—being aware of what's going on and pulling your mind back to it. When your mind goes to 'I wonder if my husband's okay right now,' you notice the thought and then you consciously release it. You can even say, 'Release,' where you have a mental image of putting the thought on a boat and sending it down a river. And then you bring your mind back to the breath. Breathe in, breathe out. Breathe in, breathe out. Notice the thought. Release it. Go back to the breath."

Michael Seabaugh goes one step further by suggesting that we not only notice the thoughts that intrude on our state of calm but label them.

"Labeling the thoughts keeps them from running wild," he said. "So just go 'Worried thought.' 'Depressed thought.' 'Sad thought.' 'List-making thought.' 'Catastrophic thought.' Notice the thought, label it, release it, and come back to the breath."

Easiest of all, he believes, is the walking meditation where we go outside for a stroll and dedicate ourselves to being in the moment and noticing what's in front of us.

"Most of the time we're walking and thinking, I have to do this or I'm worried about that or I've got to pay that bill," he said. "Instead, walk and think about that tree, the sound of the birds, the feeling of the sun on your face, the cars going by. It's really kind of amazing when you do it. You can walk down your block and see things you've never even seen before. Invariably, your mind will go to the worry, to what you need to get done, to what's happening with your husband. So you just notice the thought, label it, release it, and come back to 'tree,' 'flowers,' 'pink.' Try it."

I did try it. I took my afternoon walk along my usual route and noticed a cute gray-shingled cottage I'd never seen before, purple bougainvillea climbing over the fence of a neighbor, a car with a nearly flat tire, the way the breeze was playing with the ends of my hair. I also noticed that I needed new walking shoes and started thinking about where I'd buy them and how much traffic I'd encounter on my way to buying them and whether I'd find a pair in my size, given that my left foot's a little bigger than my right foot, not to mention when I'd have a chance to buy them with Michael having just been treated at the ER for yet another infection. When I realized my mind was running away with the worries, I labeled them "worrying about shoes thoughts," refocused on my breathing, and settled down.

Another permutation is the one set forth by Martin Boroson in his book *One-Moment Meditation: Stillness for People on the Go.*

What caregiver wouldn't be attracted to the idea of meditating for just a moment, right? Or is it for just a minute? And is there a difference?

"A minute is a unit of time that we think we can measure," Martin told me. "We can find it on a clock. We can set a timer to do a minute. A moment is actually not a unit of time. It comes from a Latin word that means a particle sufficient to turn the scale. To translate that into modern language, we can think of a moment as something that seems very small and insignificant but that changes everything. Which is why the word 'moment' gives us the word 'momentous'—because life can change in a moment. It has this kind of mystical suggestion to it in terms of energy and potential and drama that 'minute' just doesn't have at all."

Martin's book instructs us to start out by meditating for a minute—literally.

"First you do it with a timer," he said. "Just bring your mind to meet your breath. You don't worry about counting your breath or trying to slow it down or anything like that. Keep it simple. Drop your mind into your breathing and let your thoughts go."

What if we can't let our thoughts go and instead get distracted by them? Martin suggests we say something nonjudgmental about a random thought, like "Hmm," and just refocus on our breathing.

The next step is to count our breaths during that timed minute—just calculate how many breaths we take in to give us an average. Then we leave the timer behind and move on to what Martin calls "the portable minute."

"You just count your breaths up to your average breath count and you've done about a minute of meditation," he said. "Now you can do it when you're in bed with somebody sleeping, at the theater, in a meeting when you're bored, anywhere."

I followed his advice and started with a timer (I used the egg timer from my kitchen). It was fun! After getting pretty good at stage one, I began counting my breaths during that minute and came up with my average, which was twenty-five. I discarded the timer and did the one-minute meditation using my twenty-five breaths. I did it while I waited outside Michael's doctor's office. I did it in a movie theater during the endless string of previews. I did it at my computer when my browser was taking forever to load a page. It's an incredibly handy way to take a time-out from stress.

"What I found is that you can do quite a bit in a minute," said Martin. "And it means that you're going to approach the next minute less stressed, less anxious, more present."

I encourage everybody to visit Martin Boroson's website, www.onemomentmeditation.com, to learn more about his book. He has a video posted that explains the concept, and it's well worth watching.

Health coach Nancy Kalish has her own tip for learning how to meditate: the Mayo Clinic's Meditation app, available on iTunes.

"I highly recommend it," she said. "They spent about seven years researching how to teach people to do meditation in a very simple way. It's basically coordinating your breath with these very pleasant chiming tones. You can download it onto an iPod, a smart phone, wherever you want. It's super, super soothing."

I bought the app. It comes with a brief introduction, some "healing thoughts," and both a fifteen-minute meditation and a five-minute version. While I like the ease of being able to access a meditation on my iPhone and following along with the prompts to breathe and relax, I found the sound of the chimes somewhat jarring, even at low volume. I also felt as if I were cheating. Did I really need an illustration of a circle to tell me when to breathe? Still, the app is extremely popular and it may be helpful to more technologically minded caregivers than I.

My meditation journey ultimately took me to Oprah, the queen of all things uplifting, and to meditation teachers Ed and Deb Shapiro, who blog on Oprah.com. They're the authors of the book *Be the Change: How Meditation Can Transform You and the World*. They've also produced CDs that are available via their website (www.edanddebshapiro.com). The meditations that are narrated by Deb are especially relaxing. I loved Ed's meditations too, but Deb has a British accent and a voice as soothing as a cup of tea. I figured I should ask them for their take on the *m* word.

Jane: *I know caregivers should meditate, but we already have enough on our plates.*

Deb: Yes, but when the relaxation response kicks in, we're able to deal with conflicting situations without fear, anxiety, and hopelessness. That's one benefit. The other side of it is that when we're stressed it's very easy to lose touch with compassion. We get irritated more quickly. And when we're doing care work, that's what we've got to stay in touch with. In a relaxed state, we're connecting with a deeper sense of ourselves—a deeper innate altruism and kindness.

Ed: When the mind is still, you're able to see what's going on, know what's needed, be able to deal with people in a much more present, spontaneous way.

Jane: *Uh-oh. You're talking about* stilling *the mind. My mind does* not *still.*

Deb: I think the thing here is to not talk about stilling the mind. It's a bit like trying to catch the wind. So let's just talk about quieting the mind down.

Jane: *Thank you.*

Deb: The easiest and most common way of doing that is to pay attention to your breath, which gives the mind something to do.

Jane: *Are you guys into counting the breaths? Every teacher seems to have a different rule about this.*

Deb: Whatever works for people. You can repeat, "breathing in, breathing out, breathing in, breathing out." Or you can actually count at the end of each exhale. "Breathe in, breathe out, one." "Breathe in, breathe out, two." And just count up to ten and start at one again. If you get distracted, bring yourself back and start at one again.

Ed: And the breathing that we're talking about is through the nostrils. The mouth is for eating and talking. The nose is for breathing.

Jane: *How long should people meditate? Five minutes? Fifteen? Thirty?*

Deb: Again, they need to find out what works for them. I would suggest starting with five minutes. Then if you can do five, try ten. If you can do ten, try fifteen. But fit it in when you have a little space—even if it is only five minutes. I know people who do it in the bathroom because it's the only place they can be alone. And if you've got kids running around, do it in the evening after they've gone to sleep.

Jane: *Convincing caregivers to meditate isn't easy, though. We don't think in terms of our own well-being.*

Ed: I was teaching one woman who said, "I can't be at peace until my daughter is at peace." I said, "Well, then you're never going to be at peace." Until you're at peace, can you really be helping others?

Jane: *Point taken. But can meditation help caregivers even in times of crisis?*

Deb: Absolutely. We think about meditation as this big thing that we have to do, but it's just about being quiet and being in touch with ourselves. It's not that the situation changes when we meditate; it's how we respond to it that changes. We don't lose our tempers so often. We don't get irritated so often. Our approach to life is different.

Jane: *Let's say I'm visiting my husband at the hospital. Can I meditate right there in his room?*

Deb: Absolutely. Sit in a chair. Make sure your back is reasonably straight, not slumped over. Then close your eyes and just watch your breathing. Even if your breathing is shallow and fast in your upper chest when you start off, it will naturally go deeper the more you quiet down your thinking. You don't want to force it. It's about watching the breath, not doing the breathing.

Ed: People shouldn't think they're failing and give up. You can't expect to sit down and meditate perfectly right away. It takes time. But it's worth it. We externalize so much and it's frying us. Every human being should be meditating just like they wash their face and brush their teeth.

Jane: *Part of our daily routine, you mean.*

Deb: Right. Let it be a companion to you.

CHAPTER 21

Who Has Time to Cook a Healthy Meal? We Do.

- - - - - - - - - - - - -

"A meal should be something you look forward to, especially if you're called upon to give care. That time when you can actually sit down by yourself and eat something really nice and healthy is important."
—MARTHA ROSE SHULMAN, bestselling cookbook author and NYTimes.com Recipes for Health columnist

I'm not a foodie. I don't share the public's fascination with chicory. I don't sit and rhapsodize about truffles. I can't tell the difference between a foam, an emulsion, or an infusion. And please don't get me started on organ meats, because *sweetbreads* is simply a charming name for *brains*.

Still, I'm a food snob in the sense that I get really testy if I'm stuck having to eat a bad meal. We have a friend who is wonderful in every way except that she can't cook and does it anyway. Whenever she invites us over, I always ask, "What can we bring?" and mean it desperately. Her chicken breasts are the consistency of a TV remote; her veggies are straight out of the can, complete with the watery runoff; and her idea of an interesting side dish is white rice that's so starchy it gloms together and has to be served with an ice cream scooper.

But all my fastidiousness when it comes to food vanishes when Michael is having a medical crisis and I'm in caregiver mode.

When he was in the hospital last year, I'd come home at night and be so ravenous I could have eaten all my furniture—in five minutes. Who cared what I was shoveling into my mouth or how fast? Not me. I just wanted to eat and get it over with so I could return phone calls and e-mails, pay the bills, maybe do a load of laundry, get some writing done.

My usual routine was to stop at our neighborhood take-out place, swing past the counters, grab whatever was left, and drive home. Sometimes, I'd buy their horrible meat loaf. Sometimes, I'd buy their horrible chicken enchilada. Sometimes, I'd buy a tub of their horrible turkey chili, which was so spicy it forced me to have a Mylanta chaser.

The second I was in the house I'd pour myself a glass of wine, turn on CNN, and inhale the food—sometimes without even bothering to pull up a chair. I was usually finished with "dinner" before the commercial break.

Why was I so hungry and so promiscuous, foodwise? I'm not sure it was hunger that compelled me to eat like a vacuum cleaner. Part of it was the "What difference does it make" mentality that can come with being around sick people; there's this defeatist sense that we're all going to get sick anyway, so why bother to eat well. Plus, I was lonely. I'd walk into the empty house and start talking to Michael's favorite chair—the one whose cushions I'm always nagging him to fluff after he gets up. Without him at home, food was a companion.

On the other hand, I *was* hungry by the time I staggered in the door at night. I tried to eat lunch in the hospital cafeteria, but shouldn't a medical facility serve hot menu items that don't make you feel like having a cardiologist on standby? Buttermilk Fried Chicken swimming in a stainless-steel vat of grease doesn't sound heart-healthy to me. Yes, they had a salad bar too, and I should have availed myself of it, but the cauliflower florets had brown spots on them and the cherry tomatoes were as hard as golf balls, and who really likes alfalfa sprouts anyway? And then there was the soup that sat in the pot for hours; I'd ladle some into a Styrofoam cup and have to skim the fat off the top.

In many cases, stressed-out caregivers either overeat or don't eat at all, and if they do eat it's usually junk. My excuse for not cooking something good for myself when I got home was the old "I don't have the time." But would I have had the time if I'd had more in the refrigerator than a quart of milk, a jar of Dijon mustard, and a box of Arm & Hammer baking soda?

"When my son was in the hospital last year for pneumonia," said Martha Rose Shulman, the bestselling cookbook author who writes the Recipes for Health column on the *New York Times'* website, "I didn't get home until ten o'clock at night. I was starving. I took a piece of bread, toasted it, and then I poached an egg and made a panini. I had some old mushrooms around and piled them on top. It so hit the spot—just delicious. And it only took me ten minutes to cook. As long as you've got the stuff in your house, you can make a good meal in no time."

The trick, of course, is to have the stuff in your house. And by "stuff," Martha means a decent pantry.

"Start with a good loaf of bread, some eggs, and a can of tuna fish," she suggested. "But most of all, caregivers have to think in terms of devoting time once a week so that they have things done ahead. And that doesn't even mean whole dishes. It means going to the market and buying a bunch of greens. Come home, clean the greens, blanch them, squeeze the water out of them, and put them in the refrigerator in a covered bowl, not a plastic bag, so they'll last longer. Like with beets. Go to the market and buy some. Roast the beets and they're done. Blanch the greens and they're done. Then you can make a frittata or an omelet in a minute."

"And you can always buy lettuce you don't have to wash," she went on. "So make a salad and then beef it up with a boiled egg or some nuts or cheese and throw a can of tuna fish on it and it'll be a really composed dish. That's one of my favorite things to do when I'm short on time. Soups are another good idea. They can be made ahead and kept in the freezer in small containers and reheated in the microwave."

Martha convinced me not only that I didn't have to resort to nasty take-out food during periods of caregiving, but also that sitting down and eating a healthy, leisurely meal by myself could be a source of pleasure.

She believes that eating well means eating nutritiously, as her column on NYTimes.com attests. But what's wrong with sitting down with a bucket of mashed potatoes instead of steamed greens? Is nutrition really that important to our ability to get through the day or is it just the latest food fad? Do we really have to eat kale?

I consulted an expert on the subject. Marci Anderson is a Cambridge, Massachusetts-based nutritionist and registered dietician who helps people make nourishing food choices.

Jane: *So what are the benefits of eating nutritiously?*

Marci: Sometimes people forget that the nutrition that we put into our bodies is the fuel that makes us go. When we eat a diet that's stripped of rich sources of vitamins and minerals and protein, we might be able to kind of function; our bellies are full and we're getting some "energy" from calories, but our bodies aren't able to function as effectively as they could if they were getting great sources.

Jane: *Many caregivers spend time in hospitals, which are giant germ factories. Can nutritious foods bolster the immune system?*

Marci: Absolutely, if the foods are high in antioxidants. Like fruits and vegetables with a big variety of color, particularly green, orange, red—carrots, sweet potatoes, berries, spinach, and kale.

Jane: *Kale. Ugh. I'd rather eat ice cream.*

Marci: The reality is that people tend to eat comfort foods when they're stressed, whether it's ice cream or cookies, and those things do, in the moment, kind of alleviate stress. But in the long run you're depleted, and you end up with ups and downs and peaks and valleys.

Jane: *What about eating in hospital cafeterias? Is there any way to get a decent meal there?*

Marci: If there is a salad bar, try to complement your meal by getting some fruits and veggies, but watch the condiments. If you're building a salad ask yourself, "How many fat sources do I have? Am I loading on avocado and salad dressing and cheese?" Stick with one or two. In general, be mindful of portions and steer away from things with really heavy sauces. I always suggest what I call the "plate method." Half your plate should be some sort of fruit or vegetable, one-quarter should be grain, and one-quarter should be protein. And an alternative to the cafeteria is to bring staples with you. An apple is very portable. So are oatmeal and trail mix.

Jane: *When I'm visiting Michael at the hospital, I get really tired around three o'clock in the afternoon—just a total energy dive. Any suggestions for healthy pick-me-ups that don't need to be refrigerated?*

Marci: I'm not a huge fan of granola bars because they're highly processed, have a lot of sugar, and don't keep us full very long. What I recommend to clients is something called Lärabars. Their ingredient list is a combination of only four or five things—dried fruits, nuts, some sort of spice like cinnamon, and lemon juice. And Trader Joe's has some great portable snacks like peanut butter–filled pretzels. Throw ten of those in a plastic bag and keep them with you.

Jane: *For those of us who have trouble sleeping, what would be a good snack to have before bed?*

Marci: Research shows that if you were to have a couple of cups of popcorn—a great whole grain and very low in calories—or a piece of whole wheat toast an hour or two before you go to bed, you'd get a nice rise in serotonin, which may help you sleep more soundly.

Jane: *What about alcohol?*

Marci: Drinking alcohol close to bedtime decreases the amount of time we spend in REM sleep, so we're more likely to wake up and less likely to sleep soundly.

Jane: *And avoid caffeine. Even I know that.*

Marci: Yes. If you're not sleeping well, you start to rely on caffeine during the day and it can really interfere with sleep patterns. If you're going to drink that latte from Starbucks, do it early.

Jane: *Does the same apply to chocolate? I can't tell these days whether it's supposed to be good for us or not.*

Marci: Dark chocolate has antioxidants in it. You just have to watch the portion of it. An ounce of dark chocolate will give you the benefit without the problems of too much saturated fat.

Jane: *And it tastes way better than kale.*

After talking to Marci, I decided to dip into Martha Rose Shulman's popular cookbook, *The Very Best of Recipes for Health*, and find a few nutritious offerings for myself and other stressed-out caregivers on the go. I've since made all four recipes. They're insanely easy to prepare and they taste great—a win/win. We can do this, people.

BANANA-BERRY SMOOTHIE

Martha writes: "This is a nutritious smoothie that you can make year-round with frozen fruit. Blueberries and strawberries are packed with anthocynanins, the antioxidant compounds that give them their blue and red colors, and they're a very good source of vitamin C, manganese, and fiber, both soluble and insoluble. Add the protein and calcium in the milk, and you've got a meal. Make sure your banana is ripe, and if possible, freeze it beforehand."

Makes one 16-ounce or two 8-ounce servings

 1 large ripe banana, preferably frozen
 ½ cup frozen blueberries
 3 cups fresh or frozen hulled strawberries
 1 cup milk, almond milk, or rice milk
 1 teaspoon honey
 2 or 3 ice cubes, if using an unfrozen banana

Place the banana, blueberries, strawberries, milk, honey, and ice cubes (if using) in a blender. Blend until smooth. Serve right away.

BRUSCHETTA WITH SCRAMBLED EGGS AND ASPARAGUS

- - - - - - - - - - - - - -

Martha writes: "I eat scrambled eggs a lot more often for dinner than I do for breakfast. This dish makes a beautiful, light supper, and it's easy to throw together. To get really creamy scrambled eggs, cook them slowly over low heat."

Serves 4

- ½ pound asparagus, trimmed
- 4 to 8 thick slices whole-grain country bread
- 1 garlic clove, halved
- 1 tablespoon extra-virgin olive oil
- 6 large or extra-large eggs
- 1 tablespoon 1-percent milk
- Salt and ground black pepper
- 1 tablespoon unsalted butter
- 1 tablespoon snipped fresh chives

Steam the asparagus above 1 inch of boiling water or until tender, 5 to 8 minutes. Remove from the heat, rinse briefly with cold water, drain, and cut crosswise and on the diagonal into ½-inch-thick pieces.

Toast the bread, rub with the cut clove of garlic, and brush with the oil. Set aside on plates or on a platter.

Beat together the eggs, milk, salt, and black pepper. Melt the butter in a nonstick skillet over low heat. Add the eggs and cook slowly, stirring with a silicone spatula, until the eggs are just set but still creamy. Stir in the asparagus and chives. Spoon onto the bruschetta and serve.

(*Advance preparation:* Steamed asparagus will keep for 3 or 4 days in the refrigerator.)

OVEN-STEAMED SALMON WITH LENTILS AND SUN-DRIED TOMATOES

Martha writes: "Lentils and salmon are a classic combination, popular in French bistros. Black beluga lentils are a nice choice because they stay intact and their color contrasts nicely with the salmon, but any type will do. In the traditional bistro version, the lentils might be cooked with bacon or a little sausage; here sun-dried tomatoes add a savory layer of flavor."

Serves 4

> **2 tablespoons extra-virgin olive oil**
> **1 medium onion, finely chopped**
> **2 garlic cloves, minced**
> **Salt**
> **½ pound (heaping 1 cup) lentils, preferably beluga, rinsed and picked over**
> **2 ounces sun-dried tomatoes (dry, not oil-packed)**
> **1 bay leaf**
> **Ground black pepper**
> **1½ pounds wild Alaska or Washington state salmon fillet, either in 1 piece or in serving portions**
> **Chopped fresh herbs, such as parsley, chervil, thyme**

Heat the oil in a heavy saucepan or soup pot over medium heat. Add the onion. Cook, stirring, until tender, about 5 minutes. Add the garlic and a generous pinch of salt. Stir together for 1 minute, or until fragrant. Add the lentils, sun-dried tomatoes, bay leaf, and enough water to cover by 1 inch. Bring to a simmer, cover, and simmer for 25 minutes. Add salt and pepper to taste and simmer for 5 to 10 minutes, or until the lentils are tender and aromatic. Taste and adjust the seasoning. Using tongs, remove and discard the bay leaf and the sun-dried tomatoes.

continued . . .

Keep the lentils warm while you cook the salmon.

While the lentils are cooking, preheat the oven to 300°F. Cover a baking sheet with foil and lightly oil the foil. Place the salmon on top. Season with salt and black pepper. Bring 3 to 4 cups of water to a boil and pour into a baking pan or roasting pan. Set the pan on the oven floor.

Place the salmon in the oven and bake until the fish pulls apart when prodded with a fork and white bubbles of protein appear on the surface, 10 to 20 minutes, depending on the size of the fillets. Remove from the heat.

Using a slotted spoon, spoon the lentils onto four dinner plates and place a serving of salmon on top. Sprinkle with the herbs, and serve.

(*Advance preparation:* You can make the lentils 2 to 3 days ahead and reheat.)

TURKEY BURGERS

Martha writes: "Turkey burgers are a lot leaner than hamburgers, but they can be dry and dull. I moisten these by adding some ketchup and a little bit of grated onion to the ground turkey, and this makes all the difference in the world. Make the patties thin so that they resemble burgers. Be sure to buy lean ground turkey; if the package doesn't specify this, you might as well be cooking hamburger meat."

Serves 4

> ½ medium onion
> 1 pound lean ground turkey
> 2 tablespoons ketchup

1 tablespoon Worcestershire sauce

¾ teaspoon salt

Ground black pepper

1 tablespoon canola oil, or use cooking spray

4 whole-wheat hamburger buns

Accompaniments

Sliced tomato

Sliced onion

Iceberg lettuce

Pickles

Sliced red bell pepper

Ketchup and mustard

Grate the onion on the fine holes of a grater. You should have about 2 tablespoons grated onion (and a lot of juice, which you can discard). Place in a bowl with the ground turkey, ketchup, Worcestershire sauce, salt, and black pepper. Mix together well, using a fork. Shape into 4 patties (the mixture will be quite moist), and press the patties into ½-inch-thick rounds.

Heat the oil in a nonstick griddle or a large nonstick skillet over medium-high heat. When you can feel the heat when you hold your hand above it, add the patties and cook for 5 minutes on each side. If the patties are thicker than ½ inch, increase the time. Serve on buns, with the accompaniments of your choice.

(*Advance preparation:* You can make the turkey-burger mix, shape it into patties, wrap in plastic, and freeze for 2 to 3 months. Thaw as needed. The raw mixture will keep for a day in the refrigerator, if it does not exceed the original use-by date on the meat's package.)

CHAPTER 22

The Exercise Conundrum

- - - - - - - - - - - - - -

"If you exercise, there's a good chance that you could have quality of life at a hundred years old. Imagine that. You'd have all that wisdom and experience and still have a fully functioning body and mind."

—MIKKI REILLY, certified personal trainer and author

I've never belonged to a gym. Here's why:

✳ You have to talk to people.

✳ You have to sweat in front of people.

✳ You have to wear spandex outfits in front of people who look better in them than you do.

✳ You have to pay for the privilege of rolling all over a medicine ball that somebody else has just rolled all over.

✳ You have to act like you know what you're doing while trying not to get your shoelaces caught in an elliptical machine.

✳ You have to do all of that and come back again the following week.

I used to own a treadmill, but it ended up being the place where I stacked manuscripts and files and the foreign editions of my books. I used to have a stationary bicycle too, but its handlebars were far better suited to hanging my bathrobe. I played tennis with genuine skill, but that was before I tore both rotator cuffs, which resulted in frozen shoulders and toothpick arms and the upper body strength of a butterfly.

For a brief period, I had a personal trainer who came to my house and forced me to do crunches. For a brief period, I had a yoga instructor who came to my house and forced me to stand like a tree. For a brief period, I worked out to a Tracy Anderson DVD in order to acquire the body type of Gwyneth Paltrow. What I'm saying is that none of my attempts at exercise took.

In recent years I became a power walker. I discovered that I loved finding scenic settings where I could pop in the earbuds of my iPod and do three to five miles every afternoon. The walks were my refuge from the computer and there was no better way to clear my head—except when Michael was having a medical crisis.

If he was in the hospital, all bets were off, and I'd tell myself one of the following:

"I can't walk because I have to stay at his bedside."

"I can't walk because it'll be too dark by the time I get home."

"I can't walk because I need to make up for lost hours at the computer."

"I can't walk because I'm tired and deserve a rest."

"I can't walk because I'd rather curl up on the couch and suck my thumb."

Once in awhile, I'd take a walk around the neighborhood of the hospital while Michael napped, just to stretch my legs, get some air, tell myself I was doing something beneficial for my body, but mostly I was sedentary—for months and months while he went through one complication after another. And it cost me. I felt awful, physically and psychologically.

"People ask me, 'Why do I need to exercise? I'm doing okay,'" said Mikki Reilly, a certified personal trainer in Santa Barbara and the author of the forthcoming book *Your Primal Body: The Paleo Way to Living Lean, Fit and Pain-free at Any Age.* "But those who exercise are in better condition and have a better sense of well-being than those who don't."

Mikki doesn't buy into the "I'm too busy" routine—not for a second.

"Everybody's busy—whether they're taking care of a family member or running a business," she told me. "People have to make fitness a priority, to carve out time for it."

I started to protest that caregivers are the busiest people on the planet and, therefore, deserve a pass. She wasn't having any of it. She doesn't think anyone deserves a pass.

"We're living many, many years older than we did years ago," she said. "But the reason people start to decline as the years progress is not so much about age; it's about disuse and muscles atrophying. If you eat properly and exercise, there's a good chance that you could be in amazing condition at a hundred years old."

Okay. I'm not counting on living to be a hundred, but I wouldn't mind having a fully functioning body and mind while I'm getting there. Where do I sign up?

For starters, Mikki advises that those of us with loved ones in the hospital should change the way we sit in that visitor's chair.

"You want to learn how to use good posture," she said. "Straighten up and don't slouch. Think of your spine as a string of pearls and gently pull all the pearls up. Or think of it as you're raising your chest up and dropping your shoulders down and back—while tipping your butt back at the same time."

The next thing Mikki suggests is that we sprint. No, not through the halls of the hospital but rather outside, in an area with very little traffic. How does she define "sprint"?

"Like you're running from a tiger that wants you for lunch," she said.

"Seriously?" I said.

"Yes. Use the second hand on your watch to time yourself," she said, "and sprint for thirty seconds, let your heart rate come down for ninety seconds, do eight or ten more sprints, and finish with a five-minute cool-down. When you do an all-out sprint, your body will secrete 530 times the amount of growth hormone—the antiaging hormone—than it normally does. That's a great thing. If you're really pressed for time, use the steps in the hospital. Just run up and down."

Hannah Goodfield, also a certified personal trainer in Santa Barbara, agrees that sprints are effective but suggests that anything that gets us to move our bodies is worth doing.

"Whether you're working out at a gym or playing tennis or whatever you choose to do, it's your special time to feel better," she said. "Exercise decreases negative thoughts because of the endorphins."

Endorphins. They sound like something you'd order at a seafood restaurant with extra tartar sauce. What are they, exactly?

"Imagine that you have your favorite kind of ice cream and you take your first lick off that cone and go, '*Ahhhh*,'" she said. "That's the equivalent of endorphins being released during a workout. Or think about having that martini and going, '*Ahhhh.*' It's like having an orgasm."

Um, what?

"It is," she insisted. "It's that extra push when you're exercising and it's exciting."

Well, all right then. I'll exercise.

Hannah offered the following workouts for us caregivers. I've tried them all and they're kind of fun. I'm still waiting for the orgasm though. If anybody has one—say, during the "Inchworm"—please let me know.

HANNAH GOODFIELD'S EXERCISES FOR CAREGIVERS:

GOOD, FAST, ANYWHERE, ANYTIME

Burn 130 calories and boost your energy in just fifteen minutes with these routines. Pick five, and switch it up each time.

SPEED SKATER

* Stand with feet hip-width apart, arms by sides.

* Lunge left leg out to side, keeping right leg straight.

* With back flat, hinge forward from hips, reaching right arm to left toes, extending left arm behind you.

* Staying crouched, hop left foot next to right; then switch sides, lunging right as you sweep left arm toward right foot and right arm behind you to complete one rep.

STAR SQUAT

* Stand with feet together, arms by sides.

* Squat low, placing palms on floor in front of feet, directly under shoulders.

* Kick feet straight behind you, landing in push-up position (balancing on palms and toes, back flat, abs engaged).

HIGH-STEP LUNGE

* Stand with feet hip-width apart, arms by sides, elbows bent.

* Lunge forward with left leg while swinging right arm forward and left arm back.

RUNNER LUNGE

* Stand with feet hip-width apart, arms by sides, elbows bent.

* Lunge back with right leg while swinging right arm forward and left arm back.

SUMO-SQUAT WALK

* Stand with feet hip-width apart, toes turned out slightly and elbows bent by sides, fists in front of chest.

* Take a large step out to left with left foot and sink into a wide squat.

ANKLE POPS

* Lightly bounce off both toes while keeping the knees very slightly bent.

KNEE HUG

* While walking forward, hug your left knee into your chest.

* Step and repeat on the right leg.

* Continue with alternate legs to loosen up glutes and hips.

QUAD WALK

* While walking forward, pull your left heel in to your butt.

* Step and repeat with the right leg.

* Continue with alternate legs to loosen up quadriceps and hip flexors.

LOW LUNGE

* Step forward with your left leg into a lunge position (ankles, knees, hips, and shoulders facing forward, torso upright).

* Try to place your left elbow on the ground as close to your left heel as possible.

OVER THE FENCE

* Facing in the opposite direction to the way you want to travel, raise your left knee as high as possible.

* Rotate it behind you as if you were trying to walk backward and step over an imaginary fence.

* Repeat on the right leg and continue with alternate legs.

INCHWORM

* Assume a push-up position on the ground.

* Walk your feet close to your hands while keeping the legs as straight as possible.

* Return to the start position and repeat, making sure your hands and feet never leave the ground.

PLANK

* Begin on all fours, palms down, hands beneath shoulders, knees under hips.

* Push up and back until body is in a straight line from shoulder to heel.

CHAPTER 23

Sex? Romance? Is Anybody Getting Any?

- - - - - - - - - - - - - -

"Caregivers can be in a vulnerable state, needing the validation that they're not just the nurse."

—MICHAEL SEABAUGH, clinical psychologist

In 2010, on the day Michael was hospitalized for the fourth time in four months, his bowels in an uproar, his body bloated with steroids, his temperament as foul as the smell in his room, I got an e-mail from an old boyfriend. Talk about irony. Talk about timing. Talk about temptation.

The e-mail was out of the blue, after over a decade of silence, and not from any old boyfriend either; this was the old boyfriend with whom I'd had a passionate relationship that began after my first marriage, resumed after my second, and ended only after I met and fell in love with Michael—an old boyfriend who'd been hard to resist, in other words. The e-mail was merely a "Hello, how are you," but it nearly made me pass out with excitement.

I read it for the first time after I got home from the hospital that night. I was sitting at the computer, checking my inbox, and there it was on my screen. It might as well have been written in Scarlet Letter red ink.

I was so taken aback that I read it again to make sure I wasn't hallucinating. Had this man (we'll call him Tom) really gotten in touch with me after so many years?

Yep. There he was, back in my life, if only in a cyberspacey way, and I didn't know what to make of it.

For months I'd been feeling like a drudge, a drone, a hag, a crone, a person without a passionate bone in her body, much less an actual libido. I was a burned-out caregiver with neither the time nor the interest in anything other than coping with my husband's medical disasters.

And yet, I was vulnerable. A hot guy from my past was saying hello and I found the whole thing thrilling. Never mind all the other e-mails I had to answer, the bills I had to pay, the family members I had to contact. I focused on that one e-mail and whether I should answer it, how I should answer it, what would result if I answered it, would I be cheating on Michael if I answered it. Oh, the drama.

It was amazing how the thought of the e-mail perked me up. I went straight to my makeup case and put on lipstick, even though I was alone in the house and even though it was ten o'clock at night and even though I was aware that I was being an idiot. And then I regarded my reflection in the bathroom mirror to see if I still had anything going for me in the looks department.

I was ten years older since this guy had last seen me. Was I still desirable? Did I have any juice left? Did I even want to have any juice left?

I didn't respond to the e-mail that night, figuring I needed time to clear my head. I went back to the hospital to see Michael the next day. And because I was feeling guilty that I was obsessing about a man other than him, I said in the most blasé way, "I got an e-mail from Tom last night. Remember him?"

"Not really," he said while pressing the button that made the head of his bed go up and down, producing a buzz as annoying as a dental drill.

"A guy I used to go out with," I said over the din. Did my husband not care that it was Tom who had gotten in touch? He'd heard my stories. Not the details of trysts, naturally, just background stuff. I would have thought he'd be jealous that a man from my past had contacted me—or curious or furious or something. But he continued to play with the bed. "I should probably answer," I went on. "It wouldn't be nice to ignore him, right?"

"Sure, whatever," said Michael, thereby giving me permission to write back to my old boyfriend.

I went home, sat down at the computer, and composed about 3,000 versions of "Hey, Tom. Great to hear from you." I wanted to sound chirpy, upbeat, youthful, happy—as if my life had turned out so perfectly as to preclude any interest in him other than a friendship from afar. I settled on something like "Hey, Tom! What a surprise! Hope all's well!" Lots of exclamation points for sure. I hit "send" and noticed that my palms were clammy and my heart was racing. I was like some hormonal teenager.

About an hour later, another e-mail landed in my inbox, indicating how glad Tom was that I had responded. Then I wrote back. Then he wrote back. Then I wrote back. Then he wrote back. And so on.

Our correspondence continued for a few days, and it was exhilarating and exhausting. Neither of us mentioned spouses or encumbrances of any kind. The subject was *us*—how sorry we were that we'd lost touch and how we really should get together sometime. I knew I was treading on dangerous ground, but I couldn't help it.

I hated myself for keeping the communication going even as I felt justified in doing it. It was glorious to have a man pay attention to me, not as the old ball and chain, not as the one who makes trips to the ER, not as the dependable caregiver, but as a woman. I had no intention of seeing Tom again, much less running away with him, but the flirting was addictive. It made me feel like a dried-up plant that had finally been watered. It invigorated me. I stood up straighter. I walked with a spring in my step. I had more energy to care for Michael. I was conflicted about what I was doing at the same time that I talked myself into believing it was okay.

I should add that it wasn't as if I had fallen out of love with my husband—quite the contrary—or that we weren't still attracted to each other. It was just that he had a chronic illness and didn't feel well enough to have sex on a regular basis. Our days and nights of relentless lovemaking were over, and the new reality was that we had to pick our moments. Flirting with Tom was merely a reminder that I wasn't dead, that my needs weren't dead. Wasn't that a legitimate reason to keep doing it?

Not after his next e-mail, which said: "We really should get together, Jane. When?"

Game over. There could be no "when." If I'd really wanted to be with Tom, I'd had ample opportunities over the years. Instead, I had chosen Michael. What's more, it was the fantasy of Tom that had aroused me, not the flesh-and-blood person.

Being married to a man with an illness presents many interesting challenges, and keeping romance and sex alive is among them. I asked a couple of my fellow caregivers how they felt about what can be a highly sensitive subject, and I thank them for being so open with me.

➤ **Barbara Blank:** "My husband has some dementia so our marriage is not what it used to be. I don't look at him the same way that I did when he was someone I could be romantic with. Now it feels like I'm taking care of a child, and who feels romantic with a child? So that page has turned. Have I ever been tempted to be unfaithful? I've thought about what if. An old boyfriend called me out of the blue about a year ago. It was wonderful. He said, 'I'll come down to Florida and call you when I get there.' He never did. A part of me was disappointed. But I don't need that part of me anymore. After menopause it was finished, gone. I'm so glad I had all the good times I did, and if I took off my clothes I don't think anybody would get nauseous. But I don't look at that as my future."

➤ **Judy Hartnett:** "Paul's MS is the primary progressive kind, which means he is on a constant spiral downward and just keeps getting worse. The sex and romance and all of that are over because the intimacy is gone. And I'm sixty now and way past feeling desirable anymore. The ego that comes with flirting is so out of my life that I don't even feel like I can flirt with somebody else. If I did flirt and somebody flirted back, where would that leave me? What's bittersweet is when I see two people holding hands walking into a movie. I notice it right away and think: No one's held my hand in awhile. I probably really hurt from that, because there's nothing worse than feeling alone in a relationship. But it's something that I really stay away from thinking about."

For Barbara and Judy, sex and romance aren't on their radar anymore. But what about caregivers who still want both despite having husbands who are incapacitated? Is infidelity a legitimate option? Or is it just another type of self-medication, like drinking too much or taking pills?

"With caregivers, you're talking about people who are in a vulnerable state and need the validation that they're not just the nurse," said clinical psychologist Michael Seabaugh. "It all comes down to self-awareness. There's no easy way to know whether a relationship is right other than you have consciousness and either say, 'Oh, wow. That feels good,' or 'I'm too vulnerable. This isn't who I am.' I don't make any moral judgments about people having affairs. If a couple consciously decides it would be good for them, fine. But once you open that door, you have to even be more conscious. And the thing about sex is that it has such a chemical reaction when you get together with somebody in the beginning. It's a high. You don't want to rob yourself of the pleasure of that, but you can start doing things that bring damage to others and that shouldn't be the goal."

Psychotherapist Tina B. Tessina isn't making any moral judgments either, because she agrees that the subject is a thorny one.

"Often the person who needs care isn't capable of sexual connection anymore, so I've had clients who've found other caregivers to have sex with," she told me. "If it's not hurting anybody and it's helping the two of you and you're not being obvious about it, it's not necessarily a terrible thing. It might even make it possible to be more tender and loving with your partner. But you have to make peace with yourself about it. You can't go into it feeling like the world's worst person."

Tina says it's not uncommon for caregivers to meet other caregivers in support groups and have an affair.

"I've seen it happen a lot," she told me. "They have that bond, that shared experience, and they can be kind to each other about it. People on the outside tend to be a lot more judgmental. The bottom line is we're human beings. We have needs."

One of the members of our caregiver roundtable, Karen Prince, found romance with another caregiver after her husband, Andy, died. She sounds like a love-struck teenager when she talks about her new boyfriend.

"He sounds like a teenager too and he's seventy-eight!" she said with a giggle. "You should see the Valentine card he got me."

Karen met her guy at Cottage Hospital in Santa Barbara, where both she and Andy volunteered.

"He used to come in all the time, so Andy and I both knew him," she said. "He talked to us about his wife, who had MS. He took care of her for many years until she passed away two months before Andy did. I had no thoughts of him other than he was a friend who had lost his wife."

So what changed? Who made the first move? Did sparks fly right away? Inquiring minds wanted to know.

"Once I decided to go back to the swim group after Andy died, I found that he was playing volleyball there too," said Karen. "He asked me if I'd like to go to lunch sometime to learn about each other a bit. We were just friends then, although in my mind I was hoping it was more than that."

Harold Schwartz, who lost his son to ALS and his wife to Parkinson's, now has a girlfriend and seems ecstatic.

"After my wife died people kept saying, 'A lot of women will be after you. The word is out there,'" he told me. "I didn't know what they were talking about and I wasn't receptive. I was eighty years old and not ready to socialize that way. Finally, I called some friends and said, 'Are you doing anything Friday night?' They said, 'As a matter of fact, we're going out with a few couples and there's one single woman.' I went. I took the woman home and that was it. I told my friends, 'Joan was very nice but I'm not ready to go out.'"

Was it that Harold wanted more time to adjust to the idea of dating? Was he still grieving for his wife? Or was it simply that he needed the kind of nudge that women are so good at?

"What happened," he said, "was that Joan called and asked if I wanted to join her and a few friends for dinner. I said yes. We hit it off this time. We've been going together pretty much since then."

Linda Dano, on the other hand, says she can't bring herself to think about other men; her love for her husband, Frank, is still so powerful.

"Everybody wants me to date and I have zero interest, even though it's been almost seven years," she said. "When asked if I'm married, I say yes. In my mind I am. My friends say, 'You're so full of life. You shouldn't be alone.' They're right. But my life is good. I just miss my husband."

I told Linda about a writer friend in California whose husband died several years ago. This friend doubted that she'd find love again, but thanks to Facebook, she began a communication with a man who lived on the East Coast. They discovered they had more in common than books, decided to meet and, soon after, fell in love. They were married a few months ago.

"I never expected this," said my friend. "But I'm so happy."

Caregivers deserve happiness anywhere they can find it.

CHAPTER 24

When to See a Shrink

- - - - - - - - - - - - - -

"If your friend says, 'I'm worried about you.
You don't seem like yourself,' that's a warning sign."

—TINA B. TESSINA, psychotherapist

Therapists were all the rage when I lived in Manhattan in the '70s and '80s and worked in book publishing. There were the married therapists, Mildred Newman and Bernard Berkowitz, who wrote *How to Be Your Own Best Friend.* There was talk show therapist Wayne Dyer and his *Your Erroneous Zones.* And there was psychiatrist Thomas Harris whose *I'm OK, You're OK* popularized something called "transactional analysis," which sent legions of people back to the couch to talk about their childhoods. Shrinks were as prevalent in New York as a black wardrobe.

I ventured into therapy after my first marriage broke up. I don't remember being especially depressed about the divorce, although that might be revisionist history. I do remember spending a lot of time—years, in fact—sitting in therapists' offices discussing my tendency to fall in love at the drop of a hat, my tendency to discard the old love object as soon as a new one presented itself, and my tendency to feel a tremendous amount of guilt over my conduct. In addition to getting to the bottom of all those tendencies, I uncovered my fear of abandonment, which resulted in my fear of losing control, which resulted in my fear of displeasing people, which resulted in my fear of telling my therapists I didn't want to come back anymore.

I thought it was all wildly sophisticated, if costly, and I learned a lot about myself.

And then I went years without therapy and had a pretty smooth run on my own. It was only after I had married Michael and discovered that I was in over my head in the sick-husband department that I sought another couch with the accompanying box of Kleenex.

My new therapist was a woman who spent less of our fifty-minute sessions delving into my childhood and more time helping me figure out how to balance my great love for Michael with the sacrifices his illness required. She didn't prescribe medicine; she dispensed wisdom. She listened with empathy and said things that were practical and clear and made me feel that I could handle whatever came next. I wouldn't hesitate to go back to her if I needed a tune-up. Don't we all need somebody to talk to? Somebody who doesn't have a vested interest in the outcome, who won't judge us, who has the experience and expertise to give us good, solid advice?

Michael has needed more than good advice over the course of our marriage. Like many patients with Crohn's, he's prone to depression.

I remember the first time he sank into the pit because it took me by surprise and caused me to wonder if I'd walked onto the set of *Invasion of the Body Snatchers*. Michael still looked like Michael, still had his voice and his smell and his clothes, but he didn't act like the guy who had written me poetry, framed his photographs for me, pulled me into his arms and kissed me for hours at a time.

People didn't talk about depression with the candor they do now, so I didn't know what to make of what appeared to be his malaise and neither did he. He was just as baffled by the fact that he couldn't get out of bed in the morning and went to sleep very early and lost his appetite, even for foods he loved; that he had no interest in reading, listening to music, or watching movies or television; that he never laughed, let alone smiled; that he was able to work but only in a robotic way; that he took no pleasure in me.

"Do you still love me?" I asked one night when he was staring across the room, as if I really, truly didn't exist.

He turned to face me, expressionless. "I'm sure I still love you," he said in a monotone. "I just don't remember the *feeling* of loving you."

The words were a dagger in my heart. I was angry and hurt and ready to pack up and leave. But then an appointment with Michael's gastroenterologist changed everything.

"I think you're clinically depressed," the doctor told him at the end of the exam.

"Me?" said Michael. "No, I'm just tired."

"You're depressed," said the doc. "Do you have thoughts of suicide?"

Michael admitted that he did—another shocker. How could he want to end his life when we'd been so happy? Who was this person living inside my husband's body and how were we supposed to get rid of him?

The gastro doc referred Michael to a psychiatrist, who prescribed an antidepressant. The medication didn't work, so he tried others. Meanwhile, Michael started to read up on depression and educated himself about it. He was heartened that there was actually a name and a diagnosis for what he'd been feeling (and not feeling). I was heartened too, and decided that a change of scenery would surely speed the healing process.

Neither of us had ever been to Italy, so I booked a trip to Venice. Michael was a sailor who loved being on or near the water. Venice was just the place, I thought.

I thought wrong.

We stayed at a grand hotel. We took gondola rides. We bought Murano glass hurricane lamps. We drank Bellinis. What should have been a romantic adventure was a torturous experience for me. My husband was barely there. A store mannequin would have been more fun. I cursed my stupidity for dragging him across the ocean before he was up to it. Had I really believed he would just "snap out of it" if he walked among the pigeons in the piazza? But I learned some valuable lessons.

* You can't make somebody snap out of a depression.

* You can't take a depressed person to one of the world's most romantic places and think it'll be a love fest.

* You can't fix people with a chronic illness, period.

The shrink finally hit on the right drug for Michael a few months after our trip. Little by little, his fog lifted and he came back to me. He still has his gloomy episodes, but they're brief and toothless; they don't scare us anymore and we go about our business.

What does concern me is the high incidence of depression among caregivers. According to Suzanne Mintz's organization, the National Family Caregivers Association, 40 to 70 percent of caregivers exhibit some form of clinical depression.

The NFCA breaks it down:

* Family caregivers who provide care thirty-six or more hours weekly are more likely than non-caregivers to experience symptoms of depression or anxiety.

* Family caregiving spouses experience symptoms of depression or anxiety at a rate of six times higher than non-caregivers.

* Family caregivers caring for a parent experience symptoms of depression or anxiety at a rate that is twice as high as non-caregivers.

Not good.

I asked our caregivers if they'd ever sought professional help to deal with depression or anxiety. Their answers . . .

➤ **Linda Dano:** "It was at least a year after Frank died that I went for help, and it was just because all my friends were so sick of me. 'Linda, you're not getting any better,' they'd say. 'You need to talk to somebody.' I didn't want to get out of bed. I cried all the time. I felt morose. I had no energy. I had aches and pains. I thought about killing myself, but I'm Italian Catholic, so I couldn't do it or else I wouldn't see heaven. And I wouldn't go on an antidepressant because I thought the only way I was going to survive this was if I survived it fully and did not mask it.

"My therapist said, 'Why not help yourself? Do you think it's shameful to take a pill?' I was like my father. I came from the school of 'Stop that and you'll be fine.' But for the first time in my life I wasn't fine and I knew it. And what's more, I didn't care that I wasn't fine. After I started to take a pill, it was like, 'Ah, okay now.' It didn't take away the truth of what happened. It didn't make me go, 'Frank who?' But I could feel a little lighter. And then I stopped taking the pill for a while and had dips of depression. I said, 'What are you doing, Linda? Trying to show how tough you are?' I went back on it and then I was hired by Eli Lilly to be a spokesperson for their drug Cymbalta. Being out there and talking about it was tough in the beginning. But in the long run it was the best thing I could have done because it really did help me."

➤ **Cecilia Johnston:** "I went for help pretty early on. I'm on Zoloft and I love it. To me, it's part of taking care of yourself."

➤ **Harold Schwartz:** "About six months to a year after my wife was diagnosed, she said, 'I can handle Joseph, but I can't handle Joseph and the Parkinson's.' She was a woman with spirit who had lost her spirit. It was depressing. I never had interest in psychology or psychiatry, but eventually I went to see a therapist and started on an antianxiety medication and an antidepressant. I took them for about a year and the medications were marvelous. I recently weaned my way off them."

➤ **Toni Sherman:** "I was in analysis for thirty years. When my last analyst died, I was in good enough shape to not try to seek out another analyst. All the years went by. Then my daughter and I had troubles, and she and I went to a therapist together. And then my mother was dying. I called the therapist and said, 'Would you be willing to see me alone?' The idea of spilling my guts all over again was repulsive, but I went back to her to have somebody who would be able to talk about the difficult stuff that you can't really talk about with your girlfriends or your children, or you feel that you can't. And I take Zoloft. I'm not giddy with it. It doesn't make me glide through life. What it has done for me is to keep my head above water. It's as simple as that. My advice is to get every piece of help that you can."

➤ **Diane Sylvester:** "I'm pretty alert to what's going on in my body. I could tell when the intestinal things started and the migraines, so I called around and found a shrink. It was very helpful."

Psychotherapist Tina B. Tessina believes that caregivers, in particular, should avail themselves of therapy.

"You need somebody who's got some objectivity and who will let your worst self be expressed and then help you bring out your best self," she said. "You can't always talk yourself out of sadness or anxiety. Sometimes the fear becomes overwhelming, especially if you're watching a parent go through Alzheimer's and thinking, this could happen to me."

How can we tell the difference between sadness and depression, between a case of nerves and an outright anxiety attack, between a bad day and an inability to function?

"Sadness is a feeling and depression is a state," said clinical psychologist Michael Seabaugh. "You need to be aware of the difference. You need to go, 'You know, I am drinking too much.' Or 'Those Vicodin pills in my parent's medicine cabinet really numb me out.' You look at yourself and say, 'What am I doing? I'm getting into trouble.' Anxiety is an important one too. Being worried about someone is different than being anxious; anxiety is a state just like depression is a state. The classic signs of anxiety are when you say to yourself, 'I'm jittery. I startle easily and not just today but yesterday as well. My mind is always racing. I can't sleep at night.' Don't wait until the situation gets worse. Get help early."

Alternative medicine practitioner Martha Rolls Collins sees clients whose depression and anxiety manifest as physical problems.

"I see swollen joints, inflammatory bowel disease, palpitations, headaches, inflammation of every type," she said.

Psychiatrist Neal Mazer adds a few other red flags to watch for.

"Anger is probably the biggest red flag," he said. "Others are when you feel that you're all alone, when there's physical exhaustion, when there's a lack of passion in things that used to give you joy, when it all seems hopeless."

Since Neal is an MD and, therefore, authorized to dispense medication, I wondered how he decides whether or not to whip out the prescription pad.

"First, you have to establish people's trust and then figure out what their goals and strengths are," he said. "Medication is not a panacea, and you can't give somebody the expectation that it is. So it's got to be part of a process of helping to heal. Too many doctors write a script and take it to the bank. They give you an excessive dose, because they're not going to see you for three months, and they become another person you can't trust."

How are caregivers supposed to choose a therapist they *can* trust? Referrals from a family physician have worked for me, as have recommendations from friends. But what if someone walks into a shrink's office cold? What are the questions to ask before deciding that particular therapist is the right one?

"First, you should trust your own judgment," Neal said. "If you feel uncomfortable, get out. And then think about their manner. Are they respectful? If they're not respectful, you're not going to respect them. And I think it's important to ask them a bit about their own personal story."

Neal's last piece of advice surprised me. I always operated under the assumption that shrinks were loath to reveal the personal details of their lives. In fact, I remember asking one of my therapists if she was married, since I didn't see any family photos around the office, and she replied, arching her eyebrow as if I'd just asked if she was wearing underwear, "Not presently." Now we were allowed to interrogate them?

"Yes. Ask them questions," he confirmed. "If they can't share something about themselves, it's not right. You don't want a doctor who's just going to give you medicine. You want someone who will remind you of your resilience. Resilience is the capacity to bounce back, with the appreciation that you've learned so much that you would never have learned without the hardship—that there was a reason for it all."

CHAPTER 25

"Spiritual Care" Isn't Necessarily Just for the Spiritual

- - - - - - - - - - - - - -

"If you're lucky and you happen to have a faith—a dependable sort of theology that you can turn to—this is the time to avail yourself of it."
—JOHN SHORE, author, blogger, and caregiver

My mother is a Jewish atheist.

I know that sounds contradictory, so let me explain.

She's Jewish because she was born that way. She celebrates Christmas instead of Chanukah, doesn't belong to a temple, and doesn't have the slightest urge to see Israel. I think what she likes about being Jewish is the gefilte fish my sister serves at Passover.

She's an atheist because she doesn't believe there's a God and isn't the least bit interested in religion.

Yet she'll say, whenever I'm worried about Michael, "I'll pray that everything's all right." I assume her "I'll pray" is merely an expression of support, but who cares. I'll take it. I'm just happy somebody's on my side.

Unlike Mom, I'm all over the map when it comes to religion and spirituality, which is to say I believe in everything.

Do you have the name of a good psychic, astrologer, or tarot reader? I'm so there. I love having my future "predicted." It's the mysticism of it all that thrills me—the possibility, however unlikely, that there's a universe filled with spirits or forces or entities that know more about me than I do.

Is there a rabbi who's wise and kind and can put problems into perspective? I'll call him/her.

Is my local Roman Catholic church holding its annual Easter Vigil? I'm sitting in one of the pews inhaling the incense and singing "Alleluia."

I'm open-minded when it comes to religion and spirituality because I like having the sense that I'm covering all my bases. I'm reassured that someone is always listening whenever I pray.

And I do pray. I make deals with God, mostly when I'm on airplanes during heavy turbulence, but also when Michael is sick.

"Please, God," I say. "If you just get Michael through this surgery, I promise I'll never yell at him again about leaving Kleenex in the pockets of his jeans and getting a hundred little shreds of white tissue all over the load of laundry." So far, God has heard me because Michael is still alive and leaving Kleenex in his jeans pockets.

Praying comforts me. It makes me feel as if I'm not alone. It allows me an outlet for expressing my fears as well as my hopes and dreams. It's a time when I can say whatever I want and nobody will go, "You're crazy."

I asked our caregivers if they've tapped into their spirituality during their loved one's medical crisis.

➤ **Linda Dano:** "I'm Italian Catholic, so God is always in my life. At one point, when my father was deeply into Alzheimer's and I was so full of guilt about giving him the feeding tube, I sat in my darkened living room and said, 'Dear God. I know I'm punishing myself. Can you please help me?' And He answered and I mentally flipped a switch and stopped all the craziness. God keeps me afloat. I pray every day. I say, 'God, I need you to get a hold of Frank for me.' And I talk to my mother and my grandmother. I believe they're all up there and they're looking over me and helping me."

➤ **Cecilia Johnston:** "My parents are Unitarian Universalist and I was raised the same way. What I appreciate about the chaplain at the Samarkand is that she has always been accepting of their beliefs. I actually have her phone number in my phone so that whenever my parents get hospitalized she's one of the first people I call. She comes over and will ask if she can say a few words, and it's comforting. I don't know if it's necessarily spiritual or just that she's there and she cares and I trust her."

➤ **Harold Schwartz:** "I have been an atheist for a long time. I was raised in a traditional Jewish household, but at age fourteen or fifteen I completely broke away and I have been an orthodox atheist ever since. I've never felt the need for religion. I never prayed for either my son or my wife. I had no more thought of that than I would have asked the Loch Ness monster to come and help me."

➤ **John Shore:** "I write about Christianity for a living, but it wasn't my faith that got me through caring for my father. There's nothing in the Bible about having a dad you haven't seen in twenty years who's an asshole. I think Christians too often rely on this idea that if they're spiritually together they have no psychological problems. My Christianity didn't serve me any purpose other than the ways it serves me every moment. It informs my thinking. It brings me feelings of peace and I carry them with me 24/7, particularly in emotionally intense circumstances. In that sense, spirituality is everything. Faith creates a context of God. When the really big things happen you can go, 'Okay, then there's a reason for this.'"

➤ **Jackie Walsh:** "My mother was a Catholic, and I would take her to the chapel at the Samarkand every Sunday for Communion. After she passed away, I found myself continuing to go to chapel there alone. It was a source of peace and comfort to my mother and now it's the same for me."

Talk about being all over the map. Clearly, there are those who derive comfort from the spiritual experience and those like Harold and my mother who think it's worthless. But what I've always wondered is what hospital chaplains do to help both groups. Can they service the spiritual *and* the atheist when there's a medical crisis?

I asked the Reverend Teena Grant, a chaplain at Santa Barbara Cottage Hospital for over a decade, how she goes about her work.

Jane: *How did you become a chaplain? Were you always religious?*

Teena: I was born and raised in a Catholic family, but I got my college degree in Spanish literature. During the '60s I explored the Eastern traditions like Transcendental Meditation. It wasn't until my son was four that I had a moment that triggered my calling into the ministry. He had seen a dead bird the day before and he asked me why it wasn't moving. I explained that the bird was dead. He said, "What does 'dead' mean?" I said, "It's not breathing anymore. Its life is finished." He said, "Am I going to die?" I said, "All of us die someday, but most of us live a very long time and that's the natural thing and death is okay." I remember thinking at that time that I had to teach him that life was good in spite of death and suffering. Eventually I went to a seminary that required all of their ministers to do a rotation in a hospital, and I fell in love with chaplaincy.

Jane: *What was it about the hospital setting that appealed to you?*

Teena: There's a sense of realness when you're in the hospital. You're really close to life and people's masks are off.

Jane: *Do people ask to see you, or do you just show up in their room?*

Teena: They can ask to see me, but I also do rounds. One of my main jobs is to address the family's trauma—to be a non-anxious presence. Often there aren't words you can say in crisis; things like "Oh, don't worry" are insulting. So it's about not abandoning people when they're going through something horrible, so they don't feel alone.

Jane: *So you walk into a room and do what?*

Teena: I walk in and say, "I'm Teena, one of the chaplains here." Then I'll kind of wait to see what comes up and go with that. I might lead people to talk about their loved one, and they'll say beautiful things and tell stories. Or I might affirm them as a group and say they're doing a great job of being supportive. Sometimes people want prayer, so we'll all circle around and hold hands. Prayer is about asking for something greater than ourselves. It's a language that comes from the deepest part of us—beyond the chatter.

Jane: *What if the people in the room aren't religious?*

Teena: Everybody is searching for ways of coping. I'm there to help in whatever tradition they're comfortable with. We'll bring in music. We do healing touch—whatever helps them cope.

Jane: *What's healing touch? Sounds very New Agey.*

Teena: It's energy therapy. I put on relaxing music. Then I do a guided visualization to get you to be present and clear in your mind of all your worries. Then there's the pattern of putting the hands on the body or just above the body. I start with the feet and follow the chakras all the way up to the head. It takes about a half hour.

Jane: *Chakras? Wow. Very different from what I expected from a chaplain. I'm assuming most of what you do is more "mainstream"?*

Teena: When people are in crisis they lose hope. A big part of my job is to say, "Then let me carry it for you until you can find it again." Another part of my job is to help people find meaning in what they're going through. Otherwise their suffering is wasted.

Jane: *What sort of "meaning"?*

Teena: Like in a dysfunctional family where they can find forgiveness. It's such a cliché that love conquers all, but it's really true. The devotion that people exhibit is extraordinary. Some families bring thirty people to the hospital. It's like they're saying, "Hard stuff is happening, but we will stand with each other until we get through this." There was one time when the family spokesperson had to make a difficult decision about the patient and sign a document. He got up to sign the document and every single person in the family stood behind him and put their initials next to his. That was a joyous moment.

Jane: *What about after the patient dies? How do you help people who are grieving the loss of a loved one?*

Teena: Sometimes they want time alone to say what they need to say to the person who has died. I was with somebody the other day that didn't want to be alone. He said his goodbyes, and then I walked him all the way to his car. People feel empty. They'll say, "What do I do now? He took care of all the bills. I don't know how to do anything for myself." I affirm them and say, "You'd be surprised. You're going to find strength you didn't know you had. I saw how you handled this."

Jane: *So the next time Michael is in the hospital—and I hope it doesn't happen for a very long time, obviously—I'll call and ask you to come. How would you pray for us?*

Teena: I'd say, "Loving God, I know that you're here in this room right now with both Jane and Michael. And you know more than any of us the depth of feeling that's in Jane's heart right now. You know what she's going through. You know her anxiety. We just ask that you help her right now to lift that anxiety from her, help her to find her own strength in knowing that there is a way through this time, that healing is possible. And we ask for your healing presence with Michael. Bring him what he needs right now to feel your healing presence in his mind and his body and his spirit and for Jane to feel your healing presence in her mind, body, and spirit. We ask that you give her the strength that she needs in the days ahead, to be patient, to wait in faith that all is being done for her husband, and in the faith that she has the strength to get through these days. In gratitude for the help of all the doctors and nurses, may they continue to do their best for her, and in gratitude for the blessings of their relationship that brings them together now with care and love and concern. Amen."

Me: *Amen.*

CHAPTER 26

Getting Through the Goodbye

- - - - - - - - - - - - -

"Death isn't something to be feared. It's just part of the life cycle."
—SUSAN E. WHITE, palliative care manager, Santa Barbara Cottage Hospital

My mother has sayings—homey old saws she repeats when the occasion warrants it. They run the gamut from "A watched pot never boils" and "It could always be worse" to "Never wash your hair when you have your period." (That last one always baffles me. Does wet hair make a woman bleed more, catch a cold, what?)

One of her other bromides is: "Nothing lasts forever." For this chapter, I'm putting a twist on it: "*No one* lasts forever."

We don't last forever or even for very long in the grand scheme of things. We have life spans. We have invisible expiration dates stamped on our foreheads. We go along, as best we can, and then we peter out, and so do our loved ones.

Last weekend my friend's ninety-seven-year-old father died. He had dementia and other assorted ailments, and then he took the all-too-predictable turn for the worse by falling and breaking his hip. My friend and her brother decided their dad had been through enough and instructed the hospital to administer morphine and allow him to die peacefully.

"The nurse told me he'd be able to hear me," said my friend, "so I spent an hour with him telling him what a wonderful father he'd been, how much I loved him, and that it was okay to let go. It was a beautiful experience."

Two days later another friend's eighty-five-year-old mother died. She had a stroke, wanted every possible kind of treatment to stay alive despite the prognosis that she would never fully recover, and languished in the hospital for weeks before finally succumbing to pneumonia.

"My mother was the opposite of the 'pull the plug' type," said my friend. "She liked to be in control of everything, and she died miserably."

Two deaths. Two different reactions to death.

There is no one way to die or one way to feel when someone dies.

Michael's father died at fifty-eight. They'd been estranged for two years before his dad's diagnosis of liver cancer. When the call came from his sister that death was near, Michael went to the house one last time, but his father died before he got there. He regrets that they couldn't make amends while his father was alive.

Michael's mother died at eighty. She had recently moved from New York to California to live with Michael's brother. She took a nap one afternoon, had a stroke, and died in her sleep. Everybody in the family said, "That was so like her. She wouldn't have wanted to be a burden to anyone."

My father died of brain cancer, as I've said, but I'm not exactly sure when or how since I was only six and nobody talked about death in the 1950s—not to children, in any case. But here's how my little-girl mind remembers it.

My mother asked me to come into their bedroom to say good night to him. She had never done that before. I tiptoed in, because I always tiptoed once my father became bedridden and was said to be "resting." When I approached the bed, I couldn't tell if he was awake or not. His eyes were open, but they didn't seem to register, and he wasn't moving. I wondered what was up; the occasion seemed momentous somehow. My mother suggested that I take hold of his hand, which I did. She also suggested that I kiss him good night, which I did, although it felt creepy that he wasn't acknowledging me at all. And then I tiptoed back out.

Was he dead that night? Did my mother want me to see him one last time before they took him away? Or was he in the throes of dying, soon to breathe his last breath?

My mother doesn't remember, so the questions remain unanswered for me. What I do know is that there was a flurry of activity around our house soon after the good-night kiss (a funeral? a burial? people stopping by to pay condolences?) and that Grandma Rose came to live with us for a while.

You would think that the experience of having grown up around cancer, as well as being married to a walking medical chart, would have turned me into the sort of person who constantly takes her temperature and owns a blood pressure cuff and responds to every ache and pain with dread. Not me. I never once say to myself, after hearing about somebody surrendering to this malady or that disease, "I sure hope I don't get *that*."

And it's not because I have some grandiose notion that I'm invulnerable to illness. It's just that my brain goes straight to the catastrophe, the melodrama, the randomness of death—the sort of fatality that makes it onto the eleven o'clock news.

Here are the kinds of deaths I picture for myself:

* Death by plane crash (If we were meant to fly, we'd have wings.)

* Death by lightning (I can never remember if we're supposed to take shelter under trees or run from them.)

* Death by my car going over an embankment on a rainy night, by my car being hit head-on by a driver who was either drunk or texting, by a large object tied to the roof of the car in front of me that comes loose and slams into my windshield, decapitating me (If I'm behind a car with a mattress, a chair, or a kitchen sink strapped to the roof, I change lanes.)

* Death by a home invasion (I'm thinking of something along the lines of *In Cold Blood*.)

* Death by drowning (I believed my mother when she said, "Wait forty-five minutes after eating before you go in the water.")

* Death by elevator (A cable snaps and I plummet twenty-five floors.)

* Death by mauling from a pit bull (I know. There are those who will say, "Oh, but they're such friendly dogs." Tell it to someone else.)

* Death by admiring a friend's view (I am led through the French doors of someone's posh Manhattan high-rise apartment, onto their terrace overlooking the city, and am sent hurtling over the railing—by a gust of wind or the friend's vigorous tap on my back—only to smash into tiny pieces once I hit the street and be run over by a taxi.)

Yes, I have an active imagination, so the possibilities are limitless. The point I want to make is that The End comes when it comes, and sometimes it's out of the blue and sometimes it's expected and sometimes it's quick and sometimes it's lingering and sometimes it's tragic and sometimes it's a relief, and sometimes it requires a heavy-hearted decision made by a caregiver.

Here's how some of our caregivers remember the deaths of their loved ones.

➤ **Yudi Bennett:** "The day Bob died I waited until they took all the tubes out before bringing Noah, who was eight at the time, into his hospital room. Noah went over and took out the latex gloves they keep on the wall. He put them on and started massaging Bob and told me he was going to make him better. Every other time

Bob had been in the hospital, he'd gotten up and come home, so Noah wanted him to wake up and come back this time too."

➤ **Linda Dano:** "Frank knew when the end was coming. He said about a week before he died, 'Sit down. I want to tell you something. I'm not afraid to die as long as I know you're going to be right there with me.' And I was. His heart stopped twice. I said, 'Frankie, it's okay. You can go.' And he went. And my life came crashing down—a crash I've still not recovered from even after almost seven years.

"I buried my husband on Saturday and on Sunday I found out that my mother had stopped eating. I drove up to the nursing home in Connecticut and I looked at her and said to myself, 'She's done. She needs to go.' I said to the doctor, 'I don't want you to force feed her. I want you to give her morphine.' I came back with people very close to me to say goodbye to my mother. She was very out of it but peaceful. Every once in awhile she'd look at us and close her eyes again. My friend Vivien was wearing a zebra-print scarf that I had designed for QVC many years before. As she and I were leaving, she kind of threw it over her shoulder and my mother's eyes opened and she went, 'Oh, that's nice.' Those were her last words. We all laughed because it was so my mother. Heading towards the light, she stopped to look at a zebra scarf. It's a memory that I will cherish until I see her again."

➤ **Victor Garber:** "I don't think you're ever really prepared for the death of a parent. It took me a long time to get over my mother's death. I would find myself breaking down months afterward whenever there were reminders. But I was very fortunate to be with her when she took her last breath—and my dad too. That was kind of a gift. And my brother was there. My mom wasn't really speaking then, but I think she said something like, 'It's time for me to go.'"

➤ **Karen Prince:** "Andy wasn't even in bed until his last two days. In fact, we went to a party on the Monday night before. He wasn't in great shape or anything, but he loved this fellow who was having the party. On the way home he wanted me to stop and get dessert, so I took him into the supermarket and he picked out éclairs. By Friday evening at seven he had passed away. The hospice nurse had been there in the afternoon and the chaplain had done a little ceremony for all our family and we all got to talk to him and say whatever we wanted to. But it wasn't a peaceful passing. He sat upright in bed just before he passed away and was gasping for breath. But then he closed his eyes and I told the kids it was over and he was gone."

➤ **Cissy Ross:** "It's a biggie when you're in charge of making those life-and-death decisions, even though I was completely confident that I made all the decisions my mother would have wanted. She was strictly business; she paid for her cremation when she was in her fifties. But it doesn't make it any easier when you're at the hospital and you have to say, 'No. I'm not doing anything.' Watching other people go through the end is a real consolation when it's your turn. I'd seen Jackie and her husband do it. Now it was my turn to sit in the room with my mother. I talked to her and tried to keep it fairly tranquil. It was not the dirge I'd expected."

➤ **Toni Sherman:** "After my mother was diagnosed and came home with hospice, she lasted about three months. It was grippingly hard. She never spoke about death. And she never said, 'I've loved you so much, and the idea of leaving you is so painful to me,' which is what I wanted to hear so badly. The night she was dying I finally started crying. I've always had conflicted feelings about my mother. I couldn't say, 'I love you.' The most I could say was, 'You've been such a good mom.' And she said something to the effect of, 'You've grown up well.'"

➤ **Diane Sylvester:** "From the day I was born my mother brainwashed me to the fact that I always had to go beyond the medical procedures, do more than necessary to stay alive. Every time somebody would pull the tubes she would say, 'Oh, they shouldn't have done that!' So it was harder for me to make those decisions when it was her time."

➤ **Jackie Walsh:** "When my mother had her stroke, the doctor said, 'What do you want to do?' I said, 'What are her chances?' He said, 'We can do as much as you want but she will probably never be able to speak or eat or feed herself.' I said, 'That's no quality of life.' She was just a couple of months shy of her ninety-eighth birthday. She had her quantity of life. I lay down in bed with her and told her what a good mother she'd been and how it was okay to go. She had fought long enough. An hour later she was gone."

How can we make death less of a struggle for those who are dying? How can we make death less heartbreaking for those who are left behind? Is there anything positive to say on this matter—anything at all?

Yes, I think there is. When I was a kid, death was this deep, dark, scary subject nobody wanted to talk about. Now, people not only talk about it but they prepare for it—the caregivers, the patients, and the medical establishment. We know what to do when somebody is about to die. We have resources and options and compassionate professionals with specialties that didn't exist when my father was sick.

I interviewed two of those professionals for this book. Each woman in her own way has made it her life's work to cushion the blow of losing a loved one.

With over twenty years' experience as a nurse in critical care and pain management, Susan E. White is now the palliative care manager at Santa Barbara Cottage Hospital. She deals with end-of-life situations with authority and grace, and I enjoyed our conversation.

Jane: *For the uninitiated, what, exactly is "palliative care"?*

Susan: Its purpose is to enhance the quality of life for people who have chronic and life-threatening illnesses by providing symptom management and psycho-social support to the patients and their families. We see patients in the hospital, and our nurses are certified in hospice and palliative nursing. We have a physician with us every day. We have social workers that see patients in the hospital and do follow-up phone calls to the family for a year after a patient dies. And then we have a nondenominational chaplain too. Basically, we're a consult service. The attending physician—the surgeon or the medical physician or the resident—lets us know what the patient or family need and we provide it.

Jane: *I'm still not clear about the difference between palliative care and hospice.*

Susan: Hospice is tied to a diagnosis or a prognosis; people go into hospice if they have a life expectancy of six months or less. With palliative care, you can have a long period with full treatment. We often get referrals from the oncologists for people who are newly diagnosed with cancer because they may or may not be cured, so we develop long-term relationships with these patients. We get to know them and their families. We get to know what their needs are in terms of symptoms and we make recommendations for how to treat those symptoms.

Jane: *Sounds like you provide a great service.*

Susan: We do. We've developed what's called "comfort care," and it's when there is no longer anything that can be done to treat the patient who says, "I don't want any more chemo. I don't want any more surgery. I'm ready to go." We focus on doing everything we can to get them comfortable. We make sure they're in a private room, that the family is there 24/7, whatever we can.

Jane: *How many hospitals around the country offer palliative care?*

Susan: There's a national organization called CAPC, which is the Center to Advance Palliative Care. They have developed a registry, and there are hundreds and hundreds of programs in it. Their website has a national map and people can go there if they want to know if there's a program in their area.

Jane: *What's the typical way these end-of-life decisions are made? Is it the doctors that say there's nothing more they can do? Is it the patient that says enough is enough? Or is it the family that says we don't want our loved one to suffer any more?*

Susan: It's different in every case. Sometimes, the patient has had a traumatic brain injury and is brain-dead. Then it takes a conversation—maybe several conversations—between the physicians and the family about the fact that there's really nothing that we can do, that only the machines are keeping the patient alive, that he is gone already. That's a case when it's more clear-cut. There are other times when the same thing could happen and the family will say, "I don't care. I don't believe you. We're waiting for the miracle. Keep going and do everything, everything, everything." That's very difficult.

Jane: *But I understand their motivation. There must be a lot of conflict that goes along with making such a huge decision.*

Susan: Yes, and we've seen a lot of people who have had broken family relationships. They hear Mom is dying and they cannot accept it. They say, "Do everything possible." And it's coming from their need to try to fix whatever it is that was broken. But even when you know it's the right thing to do, there is always a niggling doubt in your mind: Am I doing the right thing? It was the same for me, and I do this for a living.

Jane: *What happened in your case?*

Susan: Two and a half years ago, I asked for palliative care for my father. He had end-stage dementia and was wheelchair bound in a nursing home and had his third or fourth bout of pneumonia. They thought he had a heart attack and they were going to send him down for a procedure, and I said, "Why? He's eighty-eight years old. Why are we doing this?" He died several days later very comfortably. And then I took care of my mother for the last three months of her life, so I was a caregiver. I can tell you that I have never ever gotten to the level of fatigue and exhaustion as I did taking care of my mom. I couldn't talk. I couldn't even put words together.

Jane: *Welcome to one of the reasons for this book. Caregiving is not a walk in the park.*

Susan: No, it isn't. That's why we spend so much time talking to families. We get them connected with hospice counseling for anticipatory grief. We get kids connected with grief groups. We try to move them towards acceptance or a decision they can live with. It is a process— a sacred moment—and we have to allow it to play out.

Jane: *How do you stay positive when you're surrounded by death? Are there moments of joy for you in this work?*

Susan: Oh, yeah. There are the patients that are so miserable with their symptoms, and then we come in and are able to make a huge difference by making them comfortable. That's always rewarding. And then there are the people you remember because they're special in some way.

One of my very favorite patient stories involves a husband and wife who were in their eighties. The first time I saw her I thought, *Holy cow.* She was dressed so inappropriately for an eighty-year-old in this black velvet floppy hat, a jeans jacket, and a little skirt that came to her knees and had pink hearts all over it. They were homeless. He was driving them up and down the coast in their van, and he had been having pain in his shoulders. They got an x-ray and were told it was probably cancer, but they didn't do anything about it. By the time they ended up here he had severe pain.

We got his pain under control and it turned out he had widely metastatic cancer and died within a couple of weeks. They had no money, so we were talking to her about what to do. We gave her this little list of the mortuaries and the costs of cremation and all of that. She took one look at it and put it right in the trashcan. She said, "What would happen if I just left him here?" I said, "Well, let me look into that." We found out that his remains could become property of the county, and they would take care of cremating him and spreading his ashes at sea. I said, "But what are you going to do now?"

She said, "I have a brother who lives in Oregon, so if I could get there I can stay with him and I'll be okay." We got her a taxi voucher to get her down to the train station. She was able—I don't know how—to have enough money to get on the train and go to Oregon. About two weeks later we got this card from her, and in her big flowery handwriting she thanked us for everything we had done for her and for making the last couple of weeks of her husband's life as good as it could be. It was very satisfying to be there for both of them.

Jane: *Do you have a better understanding of death since it's such a big part of your job?*

Susan: I've seen the pretty amazing ways people pass. Some people wait until everybody gets there and then they die. It's as if they have to have permission from everybody. We tell families that sometimes their loved one needs to hear it from you that it's okay to go. And then there are other patients who wait until they're alone. Their daughter is hanging in there, staying in the room all day and night, and the minute she goes to the bathroom they die. I now understand better what an incredible mystery death is.

....

While Susan E. White helps patients and families cope with end-of-life issues in a hospital setting, Deborah McQuade manages an eight-bedroom residence in Santa Barbara called Sarah House, which provides a home and holistic hospice care to low-income patients as well as those living with AIDS. Because Sarah House is licensed under the California Department of Social Services rather than the Department of Health, they're able to offer a cost-effective, unique model—from providing medical care and controlling pain to having family members over for a home-cooked meal or holding a patient's hand through a sleepless night. Deborah is one of a kind—a nun who left the convent, married three times, had eight children, and went into the restaurant business—all before finding her mission at Sarah House.

....

Jane: *One of the amazing things you do at Sarah House is to reunite estranged family members when a resident is dying.*

Deborah: We've seen extraordinary things happen here—like the Mormon bishop who came. His first son had already died of AIDS without him and he wasn't about to let that happen with the second son. He would go from bedroom to bedroom to visit everyone. And I remember the man who lived in his van. He was gay and a drug user, and he was toothless and really tall and weighed like 105 pounds. He came to live at the house and hadn't seen his dad for ten years. One day he said, "I wish I could find my dad." We said, "Where did he work the last time you spoke to him?" He said, "In the Florida state department." We called, and within ten minutes we had him—and it was his dad's birthday. His dad said, "I'll be right there." Within two days his dad and his brother came and spent several days with him so they could say goodbye.

And I always think of the woman who was about fifty-five when she came to the house. Her mom and sister were so sick of her drug use, which had led to her illness. They had mortgaged their house to get her in programs. They were just so angry and disappointed. She came to the house and was clean and sober, so her normal, beautiful personality shined through. They walked in and saw how much we loved her and how we kept hugging her, and it made them take a second look and say, "She's our daughter again." I think our affection for residents whose families have written them off—though we aren't doing it to change anybody's mind—gives everybody a way to reassess and find the person that was important to them.

Jane: *Who works at Sarah House? It must take a special person to sign on.*

Deborah: It does and they've all been here for a long time. Nobody really leaves. And no one's a nurse. One of our principles is: Nurses nurse and we don't. We just don't like the medical model. We don't think it is, for most people, a good way to die. It doesn't mean we're angry that anybody is dying at some other medical model. We just do things differently. Like we'll be having lunch and the visiting nurses will sit down and say to a resident, "Now, how did that extra Colace work for you? Did you have a good bowel movement today?" We go, "No, no. We're sitting here talking about tuna sandwiches and Japan and being an artist."

Jane: *Is that the biggest difference between you and hospice? That you don't talk to the patients about their medical problems?*

Deborah: Our emphasis is on providing a home and community for people—from the day they walk in here until the day they die—with the backup of being sure that the medical aspects, which are largely medications, are taken care of. When our residents wake up in the morning, there's a hug and a kiss and a back rub and we say, "What movies do you want to watch?" We know the medical things that need to be done. We largely have one hospice nurse now and she comes every day. Our advantage is that we're a house, a home.

Jane: *Since there's such a family atmosphere at Sarah House, you must become emotionally attached to the residents. How do you deal with it when they die?*

Deborah: When people move in, we do open our hearts to love them the most we possibly can. And when they die, we're devastated. We have staff meetings every week and a lot of times we sit and read names and light the candles and sob. But we do it together, so our grief is broken up and supported. And if I feel a little depressed and stressed, I get some hand cream and sit down with somebody stretched out on the couch and rub their feet. By the time I'm done I feel just great.

Jane: *How does Sarah House make it easier for patients and their families to handle death?*

Deborah: One of the ways is to do a home wake. There's a book out called *Grave Matters*, and it takes you through the process. After someone dies and the family doesn't know what to do, we put on coffee and tea and they cry and we rub their backs and then we say, "If it's okay with you, we'd like to bathe Mom's body with some herbs in a ritual bathing. Then we'll put on whatever you'd like to pick out for her to wear and if you'd like to help us let us know."

Jane: *Do most of the families agree to the home wake?*

Deborah: Almost everybody says, "That would be wonderful." Remember that since most people here are cremated because they're low-income, this is the viewing day.

Jane: *So what happens next?*

Deborah: We bathe their bodies and put on clean clothes. We change the linens and get rid of all the medical stuff. We bring out candles. We sometimes put on music. We put out lots of flowers. And then everybody comes back in and we say some prayers. Then we start making food. Eventually, the mortuary is called. I ask people, "Would you like to put the white linen shroud on your mom and help your mom onto the cart?" And they usually end up doing that. They lift their mom on the cart and cover it with the blue velveteen. As the body goes out, we'll grab some candles and we all walk out behind the family. And that's how the day goes. The chapter in *Grave Matters* talks about how to work this out in your home. There are only a few states that don't allow it. Your friends can come and you can do everything that I just said. You can display pictures and read poems and play a little music with a flute. I just think it's beautiful and comforting and a way not to feel helpless.

Jane: *Do you have any greater insight into death now than you did when you started working at Sarah House?*

Deborah: I've learned what it means to listen to the dying and how to be with silence. My mom died last May. I'm still not over her death and I don't want to be over it. I drive down to the cemetery once a month and put flowers there. I might not have done that if I hadn't been here. The loss of a mother is a really big thing. My work made my mom's death a richer experience. But in general, I think people should read more about death and dying. It's a topic that's coming into its own.

CHAPTER 27

Yes, There Are Silver Linings

- - - - - - - - - - - - - -

"It's really important to acknowledge, 'This is not the dream I had,' because dreams are key. But there's more than one dream."

—NEAL MAZER, psychiatrist

I know I've referenced my mother a lot in this book, and I'm about to do it again.

Another one of her adages, whenever something off-the-charts bad happens, is this: "Out of every evil comes good."

"Really?" I'd always say.

"Yes, dear," she'd always reply. "You'll see."

For the longest time I didn't see. While I thought it was noble and brave and incredibly sunny-side-up for people like Michael J. Fox to announce that they were grateful for their illnesses, I didn't buy it. Who would want Parkinson's disease, given the choice? Who would title their book about their Parkinson's *Lucky Man*? What was the good that came out of that evil? Okay, I could buy that there were some goods that came out of it, but lucky?

And then Michael's illness forced me to rethink my mother's homily. Maybe there *were* silver linings to having a husband with a chronic illness and I just hadn't taken the time to figure out what they were. And maybe if I did light on them, I'd stop wishing that he didn't have Crohn's, that things could be the way they were when we first met, that I could let go of what might have been and finally accept what is.

I asked my caregivers if they've been able to find silver linings, moments of joy, good out of evil, during the challenges they've faced.

➤ **Yudi Bennett:** "I definitely learned to be a kinder, gentler person as a result of having a kid with special needs. And Noah has made such incredible progress. When you live with somebody you don't always see progress, but then came his bar mitzvah. My family flew in from all over the world. They were astounded. The boy gets up and reads from the Torah and gives a speech and goes to parties with his friends! At first I was heartbroken as I sat there watching him—heartbroken that Bob wasn't there to see it. But what I said in my speech that day is that Noah's full name is Noah Ephraim Schneider and that his initials in Hebrew spell the word *nes*, which means *miracle*. I consider Noah to be my miracle. I remember thinking when he was diagnosed that he would probably never have a bar mitzvah. And there he was. There wasn't a dry eye in the place."

➤ **Barbara Blank:** "My silver lining is that when the end finally comes for my father, I will have peace in knowing that I did everything I could to make his situation as good as it could be under the circumstances. I think you have to be able to live with yourself and not have regrets. I feel good about that."

➤ **Harriet Brown:** "I really learned to value my husband's strengths a lot more. I had valued them before, but I'm a quick person and he's a slower person. I'm more impatient and he's more methodical. I'll give you an instant reaction to something and he'll mull it over for a while. We just operate very differently and there were definitely times in the marriage when I would get frustrated with that and say, 'Come on. Can't you just tell me what you think about this?' I thought my way was the good way and his way was a little lacking. The experience with our daughter proved to me that I was dead wrong. Each of our personalities and approaches worked well sometimes and didn't work well at other times. Dealing with a child's eating disorder has been a long haul and it's still going on. I'm very grateful to be with a partner who's more patient than I am and can be steady at times when I'm just wigging out."

➤ **Linda Dano:** "The silver lining is that I have more of a reverence of God and His plan for all of us. I believe there is an afterlife. I believe that I'm going to see my whole family and that my husband will come for me. Another silver lining is that I'm able to sit and look at the flowers and the gardens and play with the dogs now. I never did any of that. I've reached that point where life is very precious and very beautiful. I like being slowed down. If you'd said that to me ten years ago, I would have said you were crazy. And I have greater compassion for others now. I remember going to mass one day and lighting candles for all the people I have known in my life that committed suicide. I offered up an apology to them because I never knew that kind of pain and despair until I lost Frank. I totally got it."

➤ **Jennifer DuBois:** "I learned to appreciate the simple things—the times I spent with my mother—so much more. Whenever she felt good in between chemo treatments we'd go shopping or we'd go with my dad to Key West for a weekend. Those were things she loved to do, so we really tried to make sure that we continued to do them. We had some really good times and I treasure them. And certainly my friendships with my girlfriends deepened because they really were supportive of me."

➤ **Victor Garber:** "My relationship with my mother over the years was close but stormy. She was very narcissistic, draining, needy, played into all my weaknesses, which were to take care of her and to make her better. What I actually found when she got ill and became the child was that I forgave her for the bad mothering that I'd been focused on. It completely dissolved. I just felt this unconditional love for her, and I was so grateful for that. And a couple of years after she died I missed those good days that we had together where we would laugh and she would be so sweet and completely adorable.

"It's strange to say I miss the times when she was ill, but I got great joy and comfort from her on those good days. And I learned something about her: she really was a very sweet, kind, caring person. The first time the caregivers would come, I'd call her and say, 'How was that lady today?' and she'd say, 'You know, dear, she has a lot of problems.' She was so concerned about people. And she was so popular at Belmont Village. She was nice to everybody. She was nice to the staff. She wasn't demanding. I found that very gratifying."

➤ **John Goodman:** "There are a lot of post-Cushing's days where my wife will hug me or kiss me and say, 'I can't believe what you did,' and 'I can't believe how you got through it.' I think the crisis brought us closer. She knows that when the going got rough, I was there."

➤ **Judy Hartnett:** "I've never felt that I took the easy path or led a 'normal' life. You have to be pretty wacky to even be attracted to somebody with four children. What I found out is that I can handle a lot—and that Paul absolutely appreciates that. There's a lot of 'awful closeness' between us and it's very real. You can't fake it. You can't pretend it. You can't do it for anyone else."

➤ **Cecilia Johnston:** "I'm not as afraid of dealing with the decline of my parents anymore. I also know how to set things up so that my kids don't have to go through what some of my friends have had to go through. And I've become somewhat of an expert in the area of elder care, so I get a lot of phone calls from friends whose parents are declining and it gives me pleasure to be able to help them."

➤ **Michael Lindenmayer:** "The silver lining is that my family is stronger than it's ever been. We were at a breaking point. I really thought my father would have a heart attack and my mom would go into a state of chronic depression and my grandpa would die a bitter, angry man. That was the road map. But it didn't happen that way at all."

➤ **Suzanne Mintz:** "You learn a whole lot about yourself and recognize strengths you didn't know you had. You tend to become a more compassionate person. You meet some wonderful people. You and the person you're caring for may grow closer; it's not always the case, but it's great when that happens. So there are definitively positive aspects."

➤ **Jeanne Phillips:** "My silver lining is that I could communicate with my mother through music. She and I used to sing duets on special occasions and at family parties—usually old songs by the Andrews Sisters. We harmonized very well. We continued singing with each other even as she got sick. I remember when I went to see her in Minneapolis, and she didn't recognize me. I started singing to her. It was the song 'I'm Gonna Sit Right Down and Write Myself a Letter,' which had been Mom's theme song. If she was someplace where there was a piano bar, they'd start playing it for her. So I sang it to her. I went through it once and there was no reaction. I sang it again and there was a glimmer. And the third time she chimed in with me. She no longer knew the lyrics but her harmony was perfect. And when I hit a flat note, she gave me a dirty look!"

➤ **Suzanne Preisler:** "I think I learned how to be a better friend. When my mother was sick, I didn't want to hear, 'She'll be fine.' And when she died, I didn't want to hear, 'Well, she had a good life.' I would have been the first person to say those stupid things to someone else, but when you go through it, you realize it doesn't help when you say those things.

"Also, my husband, Jerome, was wonderful and I felt like we went through it together. He would research everything and talk to the doctors if he saw I just couldn't take another phone call. I have to say that the situations with my mother and my sister were the best and the worst times of my life. I pampered them when they were in the hospital. I made sure their hair looked nice. I did their nails. I'd bring in sweaters so they could just throw them over their shoulders. It was a closeness on a level that you cannot experience from going to dinner or going shopping or having a heart-to-heart in a normal situation—a closeness that I really treasure. Another silver lining is that you learn to take your time—like with my father now. When he repeats his stories for the fiftieth time, I relish it instead of tapping my feet and thinking I can't hear the same story again. And when he walks a little slower, I see a beauty in it. I appreciate those things all the more."

➤ **Karen Prince:** "I'm stronger than I thought I was, in the sense of being able to do things that I didn't think I could do. I was not the strong one in the family before Andy's stroke. He was always the outgoing one, the go-getter. Now I had to take on that role, and I did it. Like moving us across the country to California.

"I still don't know how I got rid of most of the things in the house, put the house on the market, and sold it. And then how we got to California was pretty comical. We showed up at the airport with a wheelchair, two cats in their crates, and about four bags. And once we arrived, I had no idea where we were going to live. I found us a motel room, got a newspaper, started circling ads, and found us a place that met my criteria. So I learned about myself. And I learned that Andy and I were able to keep it together despite everything. Marriages can break up over these kinds of things. Nevertheless, I felt that that's what the marriage vows were all about."

➤ **April Rudin:** "Taking care of my grandmother did a lot for me. Number one, it was satisfying to see that my sister and I could develop into the kind of caregivers that my grandmother was to us when we needed her. Also, it was great for my kids to see me dedicated to my grandmother. They were very proud of me."

➤ **Harold Schwartz:** "I got to see how amazing my son Joseph was. He always looked forward to something, in spite of the ALS. He had this great computer—the same type of software that Stephen Hawking has. He had gotten to a point where he could no longer use his hands, but he had something like an eyeglass frame wired to the computer with a thing that came near his cheek. By blinking his eyes, his cheek motions would control preset letters, words, and phrases. He would painstakingly type and a voice would speak out what he'd written.

"He would sit at that computer for hours and write the most wonderful stuff or relay jokes and political things. He had friends all over the world that he communicated with. To this day there are two guys who never met him but knew him from his e-mails. They maintain what they call 'Joe's List' and they send out material of the type they think he would have sent out. I know he was my son, but he was an amazing person. My wife would say, 'Joseph's dying of ALS,' and he would say, 'No, I'm living with ALS.'"

➤ **John Shore:** "The dynamic that I was involved in—going to take care of an elderly parent—was absolutely unique for me. So I got to have brand new emotions in a brand new circumstance. And let's face it: giving love is extremely ennobling. There's really nothing you can do to feel better about yourself than selfless, loving sacrifice. That *is* what caregiving is. In regular life you never have a chance to give pure love in expectation for nothing. But with caregiving, you're giving and giving and giving and then virtue becomes its own reward."

Clearly, this is a resilient bunch here. What I love about their answers is that they were alert to the positives even while they were busy trying not to get buried by the crap. They confirm my mother's belief that out of every evil comes good. Would they rather wake up tomorrow morning and discover that their loved one is the picture of health? Obviously, but since that's not going to happen they did the next best thing, which was to look for the silver linings.

"Life-altering events provide us with opportunities to reconfigure our understanding of the world, because we have to actually adapt to something new," said alternative medicine practitioner Martha Rolls Collins. "And in that something new is an opportunity to learn something new and to experience something new and to deepen our experience of life. There's real joy in that."

Martha is speaking from experience. She and her husband, Michael, lost their house and everything in it when her entire neighborhood was destroyed by a wildfire.

"The fire was the absolute best thing that ever happened to me—hands down," she said. "My husband and I really got clear on the fact that we were a partnership and that it didn't matter that we're now living in a trailer that's seven feet wide and twenty feet long. What mattered was that the material stuff was just that—material stuff."

Psychotherapist Tina B. Tessina has seen clients who make unexpected connections as the result of being thrust into the caregiver role.

"One of my clients was adopted," she said. "He waited until his adoptive parents died, then went searching for his biological mother, found her, and had a little time with her—only to learn she had become very ill. He took care of her until the end of her life. It was a very bonding experience for him. He got to find out about his family history, what his roots were, what his genetic inheritance was. I also have a friend who got married and had a couple of children and divorced her husband after she found out he was a philanderer. When he became ill, her daughters called her and she went and took care of him. That was a healing time for both of them. He was grateful to her and she got to make peace with him."

Psychiatrist Neal Mazer works with his clients to get them to see past the immediate crises and appreciate how they've grown as a result of them.

"I ask people to acknowledge the power of their journey," he said. "We sign on for this incarnation in order to learn something, to experience something—not to just sit there taking."

I've decided, after talking to everybody in this book, that I'm ready to look on the bright side too. Here are a few of my silver linings, in no particular order.

JANE'S SILVER LININGS

- ✳ I don't have one of those elusive, disinterested husbands who are constantly traveling or tied up in meetings or spending hours on the golf course and who only come home for a change of clothes.

- ✳ I don't sit around obsessing that my husband is having an affair when he says he's at the doctor, because when he says he's at the doctor he always is.

- ✳ My husband knows how much I love him because even though I've had a history of bolting out of relationships, I've stayed by his side during the worst of times.

- ✳ I've gained tremendous respect for my husband after watching him suffer for years without ever once dissolving into self-pity.

- ✳ I not only overcame my aversion to being around sick people but also volunteered at my local hospital where there are more sick people per square feet than anywhere else.

- ✳ I now leap into action when a friend is going through a medical crisis—even if it's just to say, "I'm thinking of you."

- ✳ I experience more joy hearing my husband laugh than I ever thought possible.

* I don't get as mad at my husband as I used to, not even when he sheds those little seeds on the floor after he eats an English muffin.

* I have a built-in excuse to say no at the last minute to social functions my husband would rather blow off.

* I've learned that there are marriages where everybody is healthy and marriages where only one person is healthy and marriages where nobody is healthy, but they're all marriages and they all count and there can be just as much love in the ones where nobody is healthy as there is in the ones where everybody is.

CHAPTER 28

When Caregiver Becomes Caregivee

- - - - - - - - - - - - -

*"Ailments are billboards alongside the road that say,
'Something here isn't working well.'"*

—MARTHA ROLLS COLLINS, alternative medicine practitioner

It all started with a sore throat.

So what, I thought, and went about my business.

Even when the sore throat became an I-swallowed-a-razor-blade sort of sore throat, I still ignored it.

It was sore when Michael was hospitalized for the first time in 2010, and it stayed sore for what seemed like months. I didn't have a fever and I wasn't wracked with chills, so I reasoned the sore throat away with "It's very dry in the hospital" or "I must have an allergy" or "I've been using my voice too much." Who had the energy to think about *my* health when it was my husband who was the sick one?

And then there were the red, scaly patches on my face and leg that were growing ever bigger and more unsightly by the day. I didn't have time to think about them either, so I avoided looking at them.

It was during Michael's second hospitalization that year when my throat hurt so much it was getting hard to talk.

"How long has this been going on?" asked my primary-care provider during the appointment I'd finally squeezed in between hospital visits.

"A while," I said. "I'm not sure."

He sent me to an ear, nose, and throat specialist, who stuck an unpleasant little scope up my nostril and down my throat.

His verdict? Acid reflux.

"But I don't have heartburn," I said.

"Well," he said, "your food is backing up."

"How delightful," I said. "Sounds like I need Drano."

"I'm writing you a prescription for Prilosec," he said. "Take it every morning before breakfast. And cut out all foods that trigger an acid response—especially wine and chocolate. Do you eat those foods?"

Do I *eat those foods?*

I started laughing. That glass of Syrah and those Pepperidge Farm Double Chunk Chocolate Chip Cookies were my end-of-the-day treats after I came home from visiting Michael, my rewards for good behavior, my way of winding down. *They were the only two pleasures of my life.*

Fine, I thought. It could be worse. I could have been told I had cancer.

Oh, wait. I *was* told I had cancer the very next month.

My dermatologist took biopsies of the two scaly red spots I'd pointed out and called a week later to say they were malignant—a basal cell carcinoma on my cheek and a squamous cell carcinoma on my shin. The former would require the services of a plastic surgeon, so I wouldn't look like a character in *The Texas Chainsaw Massacre*, but it was the shin that was more problematic. Not only is the lower leg notoriously slow to heal, making it ripe for infection, but there's very little tissue on the shin; if you make an incision there, you're likely to need a skin graft, and skin grafts on the leg have a very high rate of failure.

"Who has time for any of this?" I said to Michael, popping a Prilosec. "I don't do 'sick.' I'm the well one."

He shrugged. "Everybody has to do 'sick' at some point."

I sucked it up and had both surgeries, and the point I'd like to make is this: I let my skin lesions go unattended to for far too long and paid the price. They were larger and more difficult to treat, not to mention expensive.

In between my surgeries, around the time of Michael's second abdominal operation, my supposed acid reflux blossomed into outright nausea along with a distended belly. I'd wake up at two or three in the morning with pain in my chest and a gnawing in my stomach. I'd spend the rest of the night swigging Mylanta and praying I wouldn't throw up.

I'd said goodbye to wine, chocolate, and anything resembling an onion, and had been eating nothing but mush. Was it really the acid? Or was it stress? Had I been keeping my anxieties bottled up to the point of making my gut sick? Was I dying?

I went to see Michael's gastroenterologist and agreed to have an endoscopy. The result? Both my esophagus and my stomach were the picture of health.

"If everything's fine, then why do I feel this way?" I said.

"I don't know," he said. "Let's keep looking."

He ordered a CAT scan (it was normal) and an upper GI test (also normal), and even sent me to a cardiologist for a stress test (completely normal). I was fine—except that I felt lousy.

"Maybe it's a motility issue, and you have a sluggish bowel," said the gastroenterologist. "It happens when people get older."

Okay, may I please have a moment to rant about the "it happens when people get older" remark?

Yes, I get that I'm not twenty anymore, but I'm not Grandma Moses either. I'm a baby boomer with a lot on my plate is what I am. I don't view myself as someone whose body is falling apart. And yet . . .

My dentist: "Your gums are receding. It happens when people get older."

My colorist: "Your hair is thinning. It happens when people get older."

My manicurist: "Your nails have ridges. It happens when people get older."

And here's what else happens when you get older: your vagina gets drier and your tush gets fatter; you don't need to shave under your arms anymore because there's nothing there to shave, but you do need to pee as soon as you feel the urge because the muscles in your bladder don't work as well and you might wet your pants. Plus, you can no longer remember rock 'n' roll lyrics or movie titles or names of state capitols, let alone various passwords. So yeah, things happen when people get older, but it's really irritating to keep hearing about it.

With regard to my mysterious digestive ailments, the gastro doc prescribed trazadone, an antidepressant that's said to speed motility. Its side effect is supposed to be drowsiness. It had the opposite effect on me and kept me up all night. I dumped the pills.

Next, he sent me for a blood test for celiac disease. While I waited for the results I went on a gluten-free diet—really threw myself into the whole thing, buying quinoa, cereal made of rice, and flour derived from garbanzo beans. The test was negative and the diet didn't make a dent in my problem. I did discover that I loved quinoa and Rice Chex, however.

"Maybe you have irritable bowel syndrome," said the gastro doc, falling back on the catchall diagnosis for digestive troubles. "Let's start you on Levsin. It's an antispasmodic."

The Levsin gave me dry mouth but no relief from my stomach cramps and nausea.

Oh, did I mention that during my odyssey through the digestive system, I sprouted two more skin cancers: another squamous cell carcinoma on my other shin and another basal cell carcinoma on my face? You would have thought I'd been bathing in Miracle-Gro.

After *those* surgeries, I went back to the gastro doc, who said, "It's time you had a colonoscopy."

I was long overdue for "the butt probe," as I referred to it. Every year my primary-care doc would tell me to have one and every year I'd come up with a reason not to. Why was I such a baby about it?

For one thing, I never forgot what happened to Michael after the God of Gastroenterology punctured his colon.

For another, I did not want anybody poking around inside my body.

For a third, I was terrified of "the prep"—having to drink gallons of foul-tasting liquid and possibly throwing up in the process.

But I did want to feel better. If having the test would lead to a healthier gut, I would grow a spine and schedule it. "Just one thing," I said to Michael. "If he punctures my colon and I end up having a bag, I want you to pull the plug."

He laughed.

"I'm serious," I said. "Those are my last wishes." And then I launched into a speech about the people he should contact after I died, the kind of memorial service I wanted, and the place where I wanted my ashes scattered (Yankee Stadium).

"It's a colonoscopy, Jane. There won't be any plug pulling."

"We'll see."

I bought the prescribed containers of something called MoviPrep and instantly felt deceived. Doesn't *MoviPrep* sound like a word associated with, like, movies? Something fun and entertaining and red carpetish?

Then I read everything I could find on the Internet about how not to throw up from drinking it. Among the tips I followed:

* Keep the stuff cold.

* Drink it through a straw.

* Hold a wedge of lime up to your nose while you drink.

✳ Exercise between drinks to distract yourself from the whole ordeal. (I came up with a "colonoscopy playlist" for my iPod; the songs included "Stayin' Alive," "Dazed and Confused," and "Rescue Me.")

It all worked, and I knocked off Container No. 1 with ease.

What didn't work was the prep itself—*not at all*. In a panic, I called the doctor's service at eleven o'clock that night and left a message to report that I hadn't been able to "void."

The covering doctor called me back and said, "Give it time. It'll happen."

I gave it time—all night and into the early morning. Nothing. At eight a.m., I spoke to my doctor's nurse to update her on my lack of progress.

"Drink the second container of the MoviPrep. That usually gets things going," she said, then added: "*This happens when people get older.*"

I wanted to strangle her.

But she was right. Things "got going." The colonoscopy was uneventful and so were its results.

"Clean as a whistle," said the gastro doc.

"Great," I said, "but then why have I been having all these symptoms?" I was relieved but frustrated too. Was it all in my head? Had caregiving made me crazy—literally?

"I'm stumped," he admitted. "We've ruled out everything from a GI point of view." He paused, pondering. "Although on the scan, I could see that you do have a very large uterine fibroid."

This was his solution to my months and months of gastro-intestinal runaround? A fibroid I'd known about for years?

"Why in the world would it be causing problems now?" I said.

"Maybe it's grown," he said. "It looks like it could be pressing on your colon and creating a partial blockage. You need to see your ob-gyn and get it checked."

What fun. Another doctor to visit. Another bill to pay. Another workday interrupted.

"Your fibroid is quite large now," said my gynecologist, nodding at the ultrasound monitor as I was stretched out on my back on the waxed-papered examining table, my feet in the stirrups and her wand up my privates.

"It's the Miracle-Gro," I said.

"Let's say your uterus is the size of a lemon. That fibroid is the size of a grapefruit. I can see it pressing on the colon, which could certainly be causing your GI problems. I recommend a total hysterectomy."

"Are you serious?"

"We take the uterus, the ovaries, the fallopian tubes, the cervix . . ."

"Whoa. Whoa. Whoa. You can't just take the fibroid?"

"It's too big. That's why your belly is distended. You're the equivalent of fourteen weeks pregnant."

"Fourteen weeks pregnant," I repeated, thinking I should have a baby shower for the fibroid and give it a name.

While I sat up, she explained that the surgery would require an abdominal incision, that I'd be in the hospital for three or four days, and that the postoperative recovery time was six to eight weeks.

"I don't have time for all of this," I said, wishing I could walk out of her office and go back to being a person who didn't need the removal of several internal organs as opposed to someone who did. What if Michael had an emergency? I was supposed to take care of him, not the other way around. Plus, I had a book deadline.

"The surgery is the only way to determine whether or not you have cancer," said my doctor as she saw me wavering.

"*Cancer?* I thought fibroids were benign tumors."

"They are, but yours have grown rather quickly since your last ultrasound and that's not normal. You need to have this, Jane."

"I'll think about it," I said and went home.

I thought about it. I talked to everyone I knew who'd had a hysterectomy. I talked to everyone who knew someone who'd had a hysterectomy. I got a second and third opinion. I went online and looked up every conceivable article about the operation along with every conceivable complication. Ultimately, there really was no choice but to have the damn operation.

Michael came with me to my ob-gyn's office to discuss the surgery in more detail. The appointment was a revelation. I sat back in my chair while it was he who asked the questions, who made sure we understood every aspect of what would happen to me, who spoke with authority.

"You were really good in there," I told him on our drive home.

"What did you expect?"

What *did* I expect? He and I had been so deeply defined by our past roles that it was hard for me to imagine us swapping them, and yet he was ready and willing to do just that.

Being in the hospital postsurgery was no fun, and I couldn't wait for Michael to come each day. But I had to laugh when he said after falling asleep in the chair one afternoon, "I had no idea this was so tiring."

"What is?" I said.

"You know. *This*."

"Having to visit someone in the hospital every day? Worrying about them constantly? Not having them at home? That kind of thing?"

He nodded wearily.

I reached for his hand, feeling a new kinship with him, a deeper connection. I understood better what it was like to be stuck in a hospital, and he understood better what it was like to be the one schlepping back and forth.

Once I was home from the hospital, Michael shopped, cooked, filled my prescriptions, rearranged the pantry so I wouldn't have to lift or reach for anything, and read me to sleep at night from one of his sailing books. He was such a kind, loving caregiver. No, he wasn't required to do the type of long-term caregiving that many of us have done, but there was no question that he was willing to do whatever I needed whenever I needed it.

I asked him how it was for him to switch places with me.

Jane: *Did it feel weird to serve as my advocate after all these years?*

Michael: It was definitely a new thing for me. Fortunately, your doctor treated me as an equal. She would look at you and look at me and answer my questions as well as yours. I felt totally included.

Jane: *You opted to have a friend sit with you in the waiting room while I was in surgery. Was it helpful to have her there?*

Michael: Yes. It's a really long time to sit there by yourself. Time slows down to a crawl during something like that and your mind can run away. It's a lot better to have someone there with you to take your mind off thinking "Oh, God. What's taking so long?" It makes you less anxious.

Jane: *You seemed surprised that it was so tiring to go back and forth to the hospital to visit me.*

Michael: It was very tiring. It's difficult to see someone you love in pain. And there's only so much you can do to pass the time. It's boring and it's frightening and it's so difficult to relax in a hospital. It's exhausting for the patient and the caregiver.

Jane: *So you were thrilled to get out of there every night. Admit it.*

Michael: No, I thought it would be good for you to get some sleep. And I wasn't looking forward to going home to an empty house.

Jane: *Was that part hard—to go home alone?*

Michael: It was eerily quiet. You go home and there's no one there. It's very jarring. I knew how difficult it would be, so I made up a big batch of spaghetti sauce beforehand so all I would have to do is pop it in the microwave. I felt incredibly prepared because of all the work you'd done for me over the years. I knew what the pitfalls were, what to expect.

Jane: *You did a great job of taking care of me once I came home.*

Michael: I'm glad. I know what it's like after you come home from the hospital. It's thrilling and then there's this huge letdown. The fatigue really hits you—not only because you're recovering but also because you haven't slept for days. And I know how slow the recovery seems for the patient. The first day there's so much to do that you're on auto-pilot. But starting with Day 2 through Day 30 it's very difficult. The patient doesn't feel like the recovery is going as fast as they hoped.

Jane: *You had more empathy for me because you've been a patient?*

Michael: I certainly hope so. It must be really difficult for the first-time caregiver to know what to do during that period, particularly after surgery because there's such a high incidence of complications. You don't really know what's normal. But I expect bumps in the road because I've been a patient. Your stitches pop. You get an infection. You don't feel like eating. You lose weight. You lose strength. I tried to be prepared for that when it happened to you, so I wouldn't get mad. I always tried to focus on what was best for you. It goes a lot easier that way. The last thing you need to do is be fighting.

Jane: *If you had a choice between being a patient and being a caregiver, which would you choose?*

Michael: It's way easier to be the patient. As the patient, you kind of just lie there. When you're the caregiver, you're responsible for everything else: shopping, getting the right foods and medicines, cooking, helping you with everything from washing to changing bandages.

Jane: *Any advice for others taking on the new role of caregiver?*

Michael: The best way to make it go smoothly is to turn yourself over to the patient completely. You have to just totally think of them. And when they snap—and they're going to—you just bite your tongue and turn your cheek. It's a difficult time. You have to remember that they don't feel well. They're hurting. So just kind of be prepared that it's going to happen. Try extra hard not to engage.

Jane: *So it's about saying, "Yes, dear?"*

Michael: It's about saying it all the time. Being a caregiver is making the situation not about you. If you make it about you, you're going to fail—miserably.

Jane: *Thank you for not failing.*

Michael: You're welcome.

CHAPTER 29

Famous Last Words

"Get recommendations from other people who have been through it. A good caregiver is like gold."
—TINA B. TESSINA, psychotherapist

Michael never asks for my advice. Well, hardly ever.

If we're in the car, for example, and I'm holding a phone with a Google map right there on the screen, he won't ask me for directions, even though we're lost and driving around in the middle of nowhere and late for whatever event we're supposed to be attending. (And don't even get him started on GPS. He doesn't believe in it. He thinks people should just *know* how to get places.)

I, on the other hand, am a big asker—"the grand inquisitor," he calls me. I don't sit around trying to figure everything out myself. I solicit words of wisdom from people I respect. I'm receptive to suggestions. I acknowledge that there are experts in areas about which I know nothing or only a little something.

When it comes to the subject of caregiving, who better to go to for advice than other caregivers?

In this final chapter, I've asked members of our roundtable, along with the pros who have talked to us about caregiving, if they'd like to serve up any tips or snippets of information they haven't already shared in other chapters. I hope their advice will be useful to those who, like me, are open to anything that will make the journey easier.

➤ **Yudi Bennett:** "Talk about death with the person you're caring for before it's too late. In the three years that Bob was sick, we never discussed it and I fault myself for that. And don't say after someone dies, 'Oh, don't worry. It'll get better with time.' For me it's more painful as the years go by. What people can say instead is, 'I'm here if you want to talk about it.' That works with special-needs kids too. We're here for each other. If one of my friends is having a problem with her kid, she can call me and we can talk about it. And if I'm busy, I have friends who offer to pick up my kid at school. That's what you need: actions."

➤ **Barbara Blank:** "Be philosophical and remind yourself that there *is* light at the end of the tunnel. And express your feelings to your good friends—as many of them as you have—so you don't dump it all on one friend."

➤ **Harriet Brown:** "There was a lot of pressure from friends and doctors for self-care. I wanted people to stop telling me to go get a manicure, as if that would make me feel better. Just as everybody grieves in their own way, I think everybody copes with this kind of thing in their own way. As a grownup, I wanted to have the autonomy to do it my way."

➤ **Jennifer DuBois:** "Once you get that diagnosis, life as you know it changes. You just can't do all the things that you used to do. You have to prioritize and let everything else go. And get help. If you can't hire someone, lean on friends. And pay it forward in some way by helping somebody else. We're all going to go through the loss of a parent at some point."

➤ **Victor Garber:** "If you have a loved one with Alzheimer's, make them feel like they're still contributing. I remember when I was moving from one rental house to another rental house. I had my mother with me for the day and I said, 'Mom, I need your help.' Her whole demeanor changed—literally. I thought, this is a real clue. I sat my mom on the bed and I would take clothes out of the closet and say, 'Should I keep this or should I give it away?' And she would say, 'Oh, no. You keep that!' She was fairly advanced by then but she rallied in a way that was remarkable. She needed to feel of value."

➤ **John Goodman:** "Technology is a huge help. I would send out e-mail blasts saying, 'Don't send me individual e-mails. I'll tell you what's going on when there are developments.' I was able to e-mail our large group of friends and family and keep them informed."

➤ **Suzanne Mintz:** "The primary goal of NFCA (National Family Caregivers Association) is to improve the quality of life and the well-being of family caregivers. The way we do that is by teaching them, building their confidence, and helping them gain capabilities so that they can function better. It's that old line about we don't give them fish; we teach them how to fish. We're trying to empower them and remove barriers.

"I would like the government to implement ways that help family caregivers financially because it's expensive and often family caregivers will use up assets caring for somebody and then it's their turn and there's nothing there. Our health-care system is built on an acute care model: something happens and it can be fixed. But a family caregiver is caring for somebody who has something that can't be fixed—i.e., it doesn't have a cure at this point in time. That requires a totally different medical approach."

➤ **Jeanne Phillips:** "Alzheimer's is not an easy thing to talk about or think about. The idea that my mother, a woman with a fabulous intellect, has been reduced to the level she's been reduced to is devastating. So when I receive a letter from someone who's depressed because a family member has it, I pick up the phone and call and try to direct them toward help within their local community. There are responsibilities that go along with writing this column, and that is one of them. You don't just let people twist in the wind. I call them and ask, 'Can your doctor refer you to a geriatric specialist?' I also say, 'You're going to need more help than you may understand now. Please contact the Alzheimer's Association because they offer support groups and caregiving tips that can prove valuable for you.'"

➤ **Suzanne Preisler:** "My husband, Jerome, and I used the Internet a lot with my mother's pancreatic cancer, and it was a godsend. When you want to know about things and the doctors don't explain them, you can find out everything. The more I found out, the more I felt in control. The other piece of advice has to do with my father. When there's a surviving spouse, we need to be mindful that while our lives get relatively back to normal after a death, theirs don't because their spouse is not coming back. So I call my father in the morning and ask what he ate for breakfast and I call him at night to tell him when there's a baseball game on. Don't forget the person that was left behind."

➤ **John Shore:** "There's no such thing as a bad emotion. Don't go into this thing thinking you're supposed to be psychologically healthy and positive. Forget all that. When you have a difficult emotion, stay with it instead of dismissing it or blocking it. Ride it. Embrace it. Find out where it came from. And trust that there's something good at the core of it."

➤ **Diane Sylvester:** "Be prepared to be sad for a long time when you lose a parent. The tears come when you least expect it."

➤ **Jackie Walsh:** "There is a feeling of loss when your parent goes. I felt like I had stopped being a caregiver, no longer doing something for someone. So now I'm tutoring Hispanic children in English, and it helps fill the emptiness."

➤ **Psychiatrist Neal Mazer:** "Find somebody else who's taking care of somebody and trade for one day a week. You'll be in a new experience, thinking and feeling and sensing different things. It'll break up the monotony of every day being the same. When you're learning about somebody else, you're seeing things from a different perspective."

➤ **Clinical psychologist Michael Seabaugh:** "I think caregivers can really benefit from cognitive therapy, which is how your mind constructs things. 'I'm an incompetent person.' 'I'm unlovable.' 'I'm a failure.' 'I can't deal with that.' It's about isolating what those thoughts are and finding ways to change them. Those old things get really stirred up—especially when you're taking care of a parent. They're important to address because they breed lots of unnecessary resentment—'unnecessary' because that was then and this is now. Those thoughts will always be with you, but you can get perspective around them and process them to the point where they're not grabbing you and constantly shaking you."

➤ **Psychotherapist Tina B. Tessina:** "Time slows down when you're a caregiver. A person who needs care doesn't move fast. But in that time there can be a richness of connection. Often defenses are down, so you can talk about things you couldn't talk about before. Take advantage of the time you have and try not to be so focused on getting stuff done. That's another reason professional caregivers can help, because having their help can get your head out of the logistics and into the connection with the person you care about."

➤ **Health coach Nancy Kalish:** "My advice is to touch each other. The power of touch is really going to help you relieve your stress, especially if you're taking care of a spouse. There have been studies that show that touching another human being decreases all of those stress hormones. Any kind of touch is good, depending on what condition the person is in. If you're in bed at night, for instance, hold hands before going to sleep. Or put your leg up against theirs. It'll make you feel more attached to that person instead of feeling that he or she is a burden."

Nancy's tip about touch resonates strongly with me.

I had yet another skin cancer surgery on my leg and couldn't walk while I was recovering. Michael, who was supposed to be taking his turn as my caregiver, tripped over a curb in a parking lot, fell hard onto the pavement, and suffered torn ligaments in his ankle, a cracked rib, and a sprained wrist. He limped home from the emergency room with a cast on his foot, an ACE bandage on his wrist, and a shrug that said, "No idea which of us is taking care of the other at this point."

We laughed, albeit while wincing. "A couple of schlemiels," my Jewish-atheist mother would have called us.

Later that night, thoroughly exhausted, we followed the ritual that began somewhere along the journey that's been our twenty-year marriage.

The ritual is this: No matter if one or both of us feels like hell, no matter if the day has been a medical horror show, no matter if the next day promises to be even worse, Michael and I get ourselves into bed, turn off the lights, reach under the covers for each other's hand, and hold on tightly, fingers intertwined, until we fall asleep.

Yes, we touch each other, connecting both in spite of illness and because of it.

ACKNOWLEDGMENTS

In the summer of 2010, I went to a Yankees game with Leigh Haber, the editor extraordinaire of my baseball book, *Confessions of a She-Fan*. I asked her what she was currently working on and she said, "I'm acquiring wellness books for Chronicle, among other projects." Within a few weeks, she and I had hatched the idea for this book, and throughout the process she was smart, supportive, and accessible—everything you could ask for in an editor.

My literary agent of many years, Ellen Levine, is as dear to me as family. The fact that she read this manuscript while she was staring down her own challenges as a caregiver made her even more heroic in my eyes. I'm deeply grateful that she's in my life.

How do I even begin to thank the caregivers who spoke to me so candidly for this book? They cried with me. They laughed with me. They were superstars. A heartfelt thank-you to Yudi Bennett, Barbara Blank, Harriet Brown, Linda Dano, Jennifer DuBois, Victor Garber, John Goodman, Judy Hartnett, Deborah Hutchison, Cecilia Johnston, Michael Lindenmayer, Suzanne Mintz, Jeanne Phillips, Suzanne Preisler, Karen Prince, Cissy Ross, April Rudin, Harold Schwartz, Toni Sherman, John Shore, Diane Sylvester, and Jackie Walsh.

A big shout-out to the experts I consulted. They took time out of their busy schedules to answer even my most elementary questions. Thanks to Marci Anderson, Martin Boroson, Ilene Brenner, Martha Rolls Collins, Hannah Goodfield, Teena Grant, Heidi Holly, Kelli Jackson, Nancy Kalish, Karen Mateer, Neal Mazer, Deborah McQuade, Mikki Reilly, Elizabeth Schierer, Michael Seabaugh, Deb Shapiro, Ed Shapiro, Martha Rose Shulman, Tina B. Tessina, and Susan E. White.

My pal Laurie Burrows Grad, who chairs "A Night at Sardi's," an annual star-studded bash in Los Angeles that has raised millions of dollars on behalf of the Alzheimer's Association, reached out to both Victor Garber and Jeanne Phillips for me. She's the best.

Thanks to all the doctors and nurses who appear anonymously in many of the anecdotes in this book. Little do they know they provided me with great material.

A special thank-you to Sandy James, a "pro" in every sense of the word. She not only sees to it that my mother is healthy and happy, but she also serves as our family's unofficial caregiver, just because she really does care.